Helping Children
with Loss

Helping Children
with Feelings

Helping Children with Loss

The Day the Sea Went Out and Never Came Back

A Guidebook

Margot Sunderland

Illustrated by

Nicky Armstrong

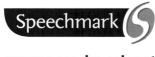
Speechmark

www.speechmark.net

Note on the Text
For the sake of clarity alone, throughout the text the child has been referred to as 'he' and the parent as 'she'.

Unless otherwise stated, for clarity alone, where 'mummy', 'mother' or 'mother figure' is used, this refers to either parent or other primary caretaker.

Confidentiality
Where appropriate, full permission has been granted by adults, or children and their parents, to use clinical material. Other illustrations comprise synthesised and disguised examples to ensure anonymity.

Published by
Speechmark Publishing Ltd
70 Alston Drive, Bradwell Abbey, Milton Keynes MK13 9HG, UK
Tel: +44 (0)1908 326944   Fax: +44 (0)1908 326960
www.speechmark.net

First published 2003
Reprinted 2004, 2009, 2010, 2011

002-5154/Printed in the United Kingdom by Hobbs

British Library Cataloguing in Publication Data
Sunderland, Margot
  Helping children with loss – (Helping children with feelings)
  1. Loss (Psychology) in children 2. Grief in children
  3. Grief therapy
  I. Title II. Armstrong, Nicky
  155.4'124

ISBN 978 0 86388 467 2

FSC
www.fsc.org
MIX
Paper from
responsible sources
FSC® C020438

Contents

This book is accompanied by the children's story book, *The Day the Sea Went Out and Never Came Back* by Margot Sunderland.

About the Author

MARGOT SUNDERLAND is a registered Child Therapeutic Counsellor, Supervisor and Trainer (UKATC), and a registered Integrative Arts Psychotherapist (UKCP). She is Chair of the Children and Young People section of The United Kingdom Association for Therapeutic Counselling.

Margot is also Principal of the Institute for Arts in Therapy and Education – a recognised fully accredited Higher Education College running Masters Degree courses in Integrative Child Psychotherapy and Arts Psychotherapy. She was founder of the project 'Helping where it Hurts', which offers free therapy and counselling to troubled children in several primary schools in North London.

Margot is a published poet and author of *Choreographing the Stage Musical* (Routledge Theatre Arts, New York and J Garnet Miller, England); *Draw on Your Emotions* (Speechmark Publishing, Brackley and Erickson, Italy); *Using Storytelling as a Therapeutic Tool for Children* (Speechmark Publishing, Brackley, awarded Highly Commended in the Mental Health category of the 2002 BMA Medical Book Competition), and the acclaimed *Helping Children with Feelings* series of storybooks and handbooks (Speechmark Publishing, Brackley).

About the Illustrator

NICKY ARMSTRONG holds an MA from the Slade School of Fine Art and a BA Hons in Theatre Design from the University of Central England. She is currently teacher of trompe l'œil at The Hampstead School of Decorative Arts, London. She has achieved major commissions nationally and internationally in mural work and fine art.

Acknowledgements

I would like to thank all the children, trainees and supervisors with whom I have worked, whose poetry, images and courage have greatly enriched both my work and my life.

Dedication

This book and the accompanying story *The Day the Sea Went Out and Never Came Back* is dedicated to Sue Fish, the founder of Humanistic Child Psychotherapy. Her work, warmth and ability to take people to the richest and furthest reaches of human nature, lives on in so many.

LOSS – WHAT IT FEELS LIKE FOR A CHILD

This book is all about the pain of human loss, and how to help children with this. Children need help with the pain of loss just as much as adults. They often need help with how to grieve.

Who this book will help

* Children suffering the pain of loss or separation from someone or something they love deeply.

* Children whose parent or other relative has left the family home.

* Children whose parent or relative has died.

* Children who have lost a really important friend.

* Children for whom their absent parent has become an obsession.

* Children who have lost someone they love, but who have never really mourned.

* Children crying on the inside for someone they have lost, when it would help to cry on the outside.

* Children trying to manage all their painful feelings of loss by themselves.

* Children who feel that they have lost the love of someone they love deeply.

* Children suffering from separation anxiety.

* Adopted or fostered children who miss their birth parent terribly.

Important psychological messages for children to hear when they have lost someone they love

✳ Losing someone you love is always very painful.

✳ When you lose someone you love, the world can lose all its warmth and colour, and feel like a cold bleak winter. But with time the warmth and colour will return.

✳ When you lose someone you love, for a while it can make you hate your life, but after a while it gets easier and the sun starts to come out again.

✳ When you have lost someone you love, it is very natural to want to cry and cry.

✳ Some people talk of 'crying a river' when they lose someone they love.

✳ It is very brave to cry on the outside as well as on the inside.

✳ When you have lost someone you love, there are always kind people who can comfort you. Sometimes it is just a question of finding one.

✳ Children are often really clever at working out who is kind and who is not; who is good at understanding very painful sadness and who is not.

✳ When you lose someone you love, it can be a terrible shock. Because you are in shock you need to be very kind and gentle to yourself, and other people need to be kind and gentle to you too.

✳ When you lose someone you love, you can feel very different inside.

✳ Memories of the person who is gone or dead are like treasure that no-one can take away.

✳ The more we have had the courage to love, the more we will hurt if we lose the person we love. So if you are really hurting now, it means you had the courage to really love someone.

Broken hearts are as common in infants and children as in adults

Loss of a deeply loved person is one of the most intensely painful experiences we can suffer. It can bring torment and anguish. It can feel as if nothing but the return of the lost person could bring comfort. And yet many people think that infants and children do not feel grief as intensely as adults. This is not the case, as we know from the neurobiology of grief (see the next chapter). In fact, because babies and children fall deeply in love with their parents, they are just as vulnerable as adults to the agony of lost love.

Detailed observation of babies with their parents shows that falling in love can start very early in life. Daniel Stern, a world pioneer in researching the minutiae of parent–infant interaction (using detailed video analysis) explains:

> My reading of infants is that they do fall in love, and do so several times over as development progressively gives them a new set of capacities with which to fall in love all over again, or 'deeper'. (Stern, 1993, p178)

> Beginning at around two and a half months, when infants begin to engage in mutual gaze, they (and their parent) may spend tens of seconds, even a minute or more, locked in silent mutual gaze. Infants do not do this when looking at other objects. Prolonged mutual gaze without speaking is a very rare event in adult human life. If two adults look into each other's eyes without talking for more than five seconds or so, it is often a prelude to a fight or sexual intimacy… Kissing is usually learned before the second year and hugging long before. At the same time children like to caress and cradle in their hands the face of a parent. When lying against or on a parent, children before the age of two years frequently make pelvic thrusts as part of what appears to be a wave of affection. (Stern, 1993, p177)

Expression of grief in infants and young children

Children and infants often give the impression that after the loss of a loved one, life is resumed as normal. This is partly because of their limited language skills, and partly because young children are still genetically programmed with powerful motoric impulses that cannot yet be inhibited. So after their loss, children will still run and leap and climb and play ball. To an adult who associates grief with sitting very still, very introverted and depressed, this high level of motoric activity seems to indicate a lack of grief. So when the grieving child is swinging on the high swing, and playing tag with his friends, parents may think, 'Well, he seems to be adjusting well.' Then, like a plane flying into sudden turbulence, the child moves into bursts of heartbreaking crying.

At other times, out of the blue, the child drops a most painful statement about his grief, his longing and his yearning into the conversation. The caring adult then comes in with empathy, but often the child has gone off again into some new motoric activity, only to re-visit his grief in his own time and at his own pace – like a bird who swoops, picks up the worm and then is off again. His timing needs to be respected. The bird will return many times. So do not be fooled because a child is seemingly unaffected by the loss. Follow his rhythm. Do not try to force him to stay with his statements of grief longer than he wants to.

James, aged three

When he was three, James lost his beloved Daddy to lung cancer. Any outsider could see how desperately in love James had been with his lovely Daddy. When James was upset, his Daddy would soothe his back and say, 'I know, I know.' Now, whenever James was upset he would say to himself out loud 'I know, I know.' Because James continued to run around, ride his bike with enormous vigour and play rough-and-tumble with his friends, observers may have thought that James had simply got over the loss of his Daddy. But as James developed more language skills, he started to refer increasingly to his Daddy. Suddenly, in the middle of a conversation about something entirely different, or in the middle of a car ride or building a sandcastle, he would speak about his Daddy. Seemingly out of nowhere he would say, 'My Daddy can't see my legs any more.', or 'My Daddy didn't want to go.', or 'Cigarettes took my Daddy. They shouldn't have.' One day, while eating an ice cream on the beach, he expressed his anger at his mother: 'You should have chosen someone else to be your husband.'

It is easy to think that a child, who is not old enough to have a sophisticated language of grief or who is still being very upbeat and active, is not actually grieving. Yet the truth is that the profound pain of losing someone he loves can be very difficult for a child to speak about. He may be able to paint a picture or play music about it, but speaking about it is not how he will express it with any ease or fluency. Children often need an adult to find the words for an experience that they may find too difficult to express verbally. A child who is grieving, but unable to find the words to express his feelings, will tend to show the grief through his behaviour. In particular, such feelings may be seen in problems at school; learning difficulties, sleeping or eating problems; nightmares; sudden angry or raging behaviour; or just a general withdrawing and cutting-off. In the next chapter we look at the reasons why these symptoms can arise.

The shock of loss that feels like it will never end

> And when you left
> I hung my lifeless life,
> Like long unchosen garment,
> In the dark belly of some forgotten wardrobe,
> *and will you know?*
>
> *Margot Sunderland*

The moment of loss – someone the child has loved deeply leaves, or dies – can herald a complex mix of agonising feelings: despair, futility, anger, fear, shock, emptiness. The strength of feeling, and the pain of the grief, can at times feel too much to endure. 'Oh to feel just the sweetness of sadness.', as Shakespeare put it, rather than this acute ache, this searing, screaming pain. And because of its intensity, children and adults can at times feel almost crazy with grief.

For adults and children alike, the pain of loss can touch everything. Even the very sense of who you are can be deeply affected. You feel you are no longer the same person. The loss changes not only how you view the world, but how you view yourself. CS Lewis, for example, found one of the hardest things about his wife's death was her physical absence in terms of his *own* body and self. He said, 'There is one place where her absence comes locally home to me, and it is a place I can't avoid. I mean my own body. It had such a different importance while it was the body of H's lover. Now it's like an empty house.' (Lewis, 1966, p12.)

And yet, once again, because children do not have a sophisticated vocabulary for separation and loss, these agonising feelings may go unexpressed in words, and so unnoticed. Only the child's behaviour – often increasingly worrying – will give it away.

The legacy of terrible bleakness

Siege

I drag about this thirst for you, your absence
Blaring out a pain of savage poverty;
My mind a stare of lack, a tomb of rotting yesterdays.
Their callous echoes mounting to a yell that throws
Its shock, its slap of loss, dislodging everything
Unsteadies everything, all hope into a slump
Of something too snuffed out.

The light, dies here.

And now you tread yourself into my grief
Like a vandal, intent to smash this too frail self
Which splinters with the thud of yearning.
No dawn, no bright of dawn,
Just some lost river, in a land already parched and black
I cannot cry you out of me.

Margot Sunderland

For the grieving child who has perhaps just lost his Mummy, the intensity of the pain and yearning can feel unbearable. The pain hits him in fits and starts. Sometimes he is seemingly playing happily, and adults worry that he is denying his grief. Then suddenly he is overwhelmed by grief: 'I just want my Mummy, I want my Mummy, I want my Mummy…', he howls and howls as if forever. Adults may worry that they themselves will not be able to stand the agony of his calling, it is so raw and terrible. It screams of an intensity that makes them remember things in their own lives they are desperate to forget. The world has a terrible bleakness and a terrible rawness, if you are a child who has just lost your beloved Mummy or Daddy (see Figure 1).

Figure 1
A reconstruction of Emma's sandplay picture called 'No Man's Land'. When Emma was seven her father, whom she loved dearly, left to live abroad with another woman.

No more Mummy

Because she's gone,
There's just the dizzy and the strange
Of too much scatter in the swirl;
So I'm this skull of flung and lost
That cannot move the vastness from its eyes,
These withered sacks for eyes which have no sight of her
In this lonely steep of night.

Because she's gone,
I cannot let her know
About the jagged bits of fall and creep
That's clinging to the chill of air,
About these ceaseless floats of speck
That push themselves into my face,
About there is no you.
And there will be no days, no days
And there will be no days.

Margot Sunderland

Some children struggling with loss are heartbreakingly moving when given art media to express their feelings. So many bereaved children express a terrible inner bleakness – the bleakness of being plunged into a world bereft of a far too precious human connection.

In this bleak world, some children withdraw more and more, cutting themselves off from warm contact of friends or other loved ones who were once sources of emotional nourishment.

Gemma, aged eight

Gemma, aged eight, had lost her mother. She no longer wanted to play with her friends. Her school work went downhill and day after day she was reported just staring out of the window in her lessons. In this place of isolation, Gemma was putting herself further and further away from the comfort and goodness in her world.

Children speaking in play therapy about the bleak world after losing a loved one

---

Janice, aged eleven

Janice's single mother left her. She was put into care. She said: 'The world's too cold. It could smash me up with its coldness.'

Emma, aged six

Emma's mother died when she was six. She told this story when she was ten.

'The sun falls out of the sky. Sometimes I feel like I fall out of the sky too. Everything lovely has fallen out of everything and got lost at the bottom of the world. I sometimes feel as if I live at the bottom of the world.'

See also Figures 2 and 3 for Philip's and Ahmed's stories.

At the age of eight, Philip rang Social Services to say that his father was violently hitting him and his little sister. The year before, Philip's mother had died. This is a reconstruction of Philip's sandplay story enacted in counselling. See how, in part, he experiences his mother's death and father's abusive behaviour as both a rejection and a rupture. Also see how he chooses the images of both defecation and bare light bulbs to depict emotional neglect and a place that is desperately unhomely, stark, bleak and devoid of all warmth and comfort.

Philip said about this image, 'The parents didn't want the children anymore so they left and lived in a tent in the garden. The garden was struck by lightening, so they knocked on the door, but Mum turned them away. So they went to the shop, but the shop was closed. Birds are pooing on the flowers. I don't like things that don't shine properly like bare light bulbs.'

Figure 2 Emotional bleakness

Ahmed is seven. His parents are both alcoholic, so he is put into care regularly for temporary periods. He 'keeps losing everything'. Ahmed said about his sandplay story, 'There's this scavenger puppet. He spends all day trying to eat chewing gum that's got stuck on the floor. He drinks from puddles and eats from dustbins. All the animals are hungry. They have lost everything.'

Figure 3

Freud described beautifully, in his paper 'Mourning and Melancholia', how with the loss of a loved one the world can lose all its meaning:

> The distinguishing mental features of melancholia [depression] are a profoundly painful dejection, cessation of interest in the outside world, loss of the capacity to love, inhibition of all activity, and a lowering of the self-regarding feelings to a degree that finds utterance in self-reproaches and self-revilings, and culminates in a delusional expectation of punishment ... with one exception, the same traits are met with in mourning. The disturbance of self-regard is absent in mourning; but otherwise the features are the same. Profound mourning, the reaction to the loss of someone who is loved, contains the same painful frame of mind, the same loss of interest in the outside world – in so far as it does not recall him ... (Freud, 1984, p255)

When the world not only turns bleak but also hostile

> In mourning it is the world which has become poor and empty; in melancholia [depression] it is the ego itself. (Freud, 1984, p255)

Some children's loneliness without their loved one makes their world seem not just bleak, but actually hostile. It becomes a cold, rejecting, unfriendly place. This often affects their perception of everything. Because their inner world is so bleak, they begin to see the outer world as bleak and hostile too. They no longer hear the birds singing. They no longer feel the warmth of the sun on their skin. All is experienced as cold and attacking – people as well as things. Some grieving children then become hostile and aggressive themselves as a result. (In the next chapter we look at how a child's brain chemistry can change as a response to grief, provoking an aggressive response.)

> **Stella, aged eight**
> Stella lost her mother when she was eight. (Her father had left a long time ago.) She told this story: 'This is a story of vases with no flowers, houses with no windows, and parents with no smiles. There is also a biting wind and people walk along with hate in their eyes.'

What are the roots that clutch, what branches grow
Out of this stony rubbish? Son of man,
You cannot say, or guess, for you know only
A heap of broken images, where the sun beats,
And the dead tree gives no shelter, the cricket no relief,
And the dry stone no sound of water.

Eliot, 1990, p63

Grieving children who move into a private, shut-off world of one

> There is a fearful gnawing sensation which chills and destroys one, on leaving ... persons for which there are no substitutes. (Edward Lear, in Strachey, 1907)

Some children withdraw from the world of people after losing someone they love. It is as if they feel that the world has let them down so badly they are compelled to move into a private, unpeopled world. Such children can feel so betrayed by this terrible life event of tragic loss that they no longer wish to take part in an active social world. These are the children who then become

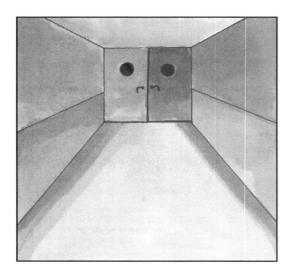

Figure 4 Grieving children can be drawn to places of desolation, wilderness and neglect as if they are in some way comforted to have an external mirror of what they feel inside.

hard to connect with and so difficult to reach in any meaningful way. They seek neither help nor comfort. Some find a bleak place as their private place of sanctuary – an empty room, a piece of waste – as if it mirrors what they are feeling inside (see Figure 4).

By way of comparison, Jane Goodall found, in her moving study of chimpanzees (1990), that if young chimps lose their mothers, many cannot survive the trauma and actually die. They are old enough to survive physiologically, but they go into terrible states of despair and stop eating. She shows tragic photos of chimpanzee 'Flint' whose mother died when he was just eight years old. After his mother's death, Flint went to sit where she had died, and then after a few days died there himself. This is a very sobering lesson for anyone who makes light of a bereaved child's pain, or is taken in by their seemingly happy play.

How depression in children so often covers a broken heart

A ... depression is a kind of spiritual winter, frozen, sterile, unmoving. The richer, softer and more delectable nature becomes, the deeper that internal winter seems, and the wider and more intolerable the abyss which separates the inner world from the outer. (Alvarez, 1971, p103)

Wolpert describes how a six-month-old monkey who loses a parent will initially scream and cry. It will stop playing, and lose interest in any exploration. Gradually, the monkey becomes more and more lethargic and withdrawn. It moves into a typical depression, as can be found in humans. Wolpert explains that some monkeys 'adopt...a motionless foetal posture away from the rest of the group' (Wolpert, 1999, pp88–9).

Depression is very different from sadness. Depression is about pain and despair, and the nightmare that everything you perceive seems coloured with harshness and strife (see Figure 5). There is neurobiological reality to all this. When cortisol (stress hormone) is way above the base rate, it can block all pleasure chemicals. This means that every perception is indeed coloured with harshness and bleakness. There is a mechanism in the brain that usually prevents stress chemicals staying at too high a level. In cases of clinical depression, this mechanism fails to function properly, so the brain just keeps pumping out more and more stress chemicals, triggering the body to pump out more and more stress hormones into the blood. This process can happen just as much in the child's brain as in that of the adult. And yet, tragically, this fact is often not recognised in children.

Figure 5 'I can't let the comfort in, so I cannot be comforted.'

In counselling, depressed children often draw pictures or enact in sandplay, places of bleakness and desolation, showing a world devoid of warm human connection. If such connection is offered, a clinically depressed child may be unable to use it. For many depressed children, this is because the only person they want comfort from, is the very person who has left them.

Depression means a desperate unhappiness, as Wolpert says, 'which shuts out every comfort and every gleam of light … Everything has become disagreeable to him; everything wearies him… Everywhere he sees only the dark side and difficulties' (Wolpert, 1999, p2). This is because when the high levels of stress chemicals block the brain's positive arousal chemicals, the child is *neurobiologically incapable* of feeling hope, desire, joy, humour, curiosity, excitement. So if a child is clinically depressed as a result of losing someone they loved deeply, they will be consumed by relentlessly negative thoughts and feelings. They cannot imagine ever feeling anything other than this state of perpetual despair.

Suicide accounts for 20 per cent of all deaths in young people. (The Mental Health Foundation, 1999)

> **Peter, aged fourteen**
> Peter loved his mother deeply. For 12 years, Peter's mother had been a single parent. Peter had no siblings. When he was 12, his mother's lover moved in with them. This man beat up Peter on several occasions. Social Services were notified, and told the mother that she had to decide between her lover and Peter, as Peter was at risk. The mother chose the lover. Peter went into care.

For two years before I saw him as a therapist, day after day, Peter sat and stared at the wall. Some children with awful stories like this, do indeed know despair. It is a terrible internal place of utter desolation. Such a child who has lost the mother he loves because she has chosen another, is truly in a veritable winter, rather like that described by Primo Levi in his evocation of an actual terrible winter in Nazi Poland:

> We fought with all our strength to prevent the arrival of winter. We clung to all the warm hours, at every dusk we tried to keep the sun in the sky for a little longer, but it was all in vain. Yesterday evening the sun went down irrevocably behind a confusion of dirty clouds, chimneystacks and wires, and today it is winter. (Levi 1979, p129)

When I started to work with Peter in therapy, his first images in sandplay depicted one parched landscape after another. They all evoked the most painful emotional impoverishment. Animals could not get to the waterhole, or were left feeding out of rubbish bins on other people's left-overs. People died of the cold, lonely and forgotten. Peter, like so many clinically depressed children, found some tangible relief in being able to show his inner world of anguish in an art image. It helped Peter to share with me the barrenness, the squalor and emptiness of his inner world, rather than continuing with the loneliness of having to carry this terrible burden of pain, unshared, unconveyed.

Emotional bleakness is also about the agonising loss of all human connection. Peter once made up an amazing story about a baby left in a place of leafless trees, stripped bare of life. It reminded me of CS Lewis, and how bleak the world became when he lost his wife. Depicting this horrendous emotional *lack* so well, Lewis said, 'Her absence is like the sky, spread over everything' (1966, p76).

The pain of no more shared experiences

When a loved one leaves or dies, the child is brought up against the awful truth that there is now *'no opportunity for sharing'* (Winnicott, 1996, p47). No more 'Look, Mummy!' No more 'Look at that Mummy!', 'Come and see.' No more, 'Look what I did.' Shared experiences with someone you love are pure treasure, and so knowing you won't have any more can be agony. The new book, the new video, the freshly built sandcastle, just don't have that special magic any more, unless shared with the loved person who's gone. In fact these things, once so bejewelled, can now seem dull and pointless.

The child who cannot bear to feel his grief

> Her cat had died but she had felt indifferent about it. As she had then explained: 'If I let it hurt me, I'd be saddened by everything.' (Bowlby, 1988, p69)

There are some children who cannot bear to feel their grief. It is too painful and too frightening. The unbearable can very easily become the unthinkable. But denial has its costs. Sometimes it leaves a numbness, or sense of unreality. By cutting off from so much feeling, these children can cut off from too much aliveness – sometimes from essential connection with themselves.

Figure 6 'It hurts too much to feel.' (Harry age seven)

This picture is a depiction of Harry's sand play after his mother died.

As one little boy whose mother died said, 'My heart's gone in my head because I'm a weird little jelly.' Very eloquently, he was speaking of a loss of connection with himself. Loss of connection with the loved one can understandably lead to a sense of loss of connection with oneself. But when feelings are repressed and banished to the unconscious, as Freud knew only too well, the cost is high.

Here are some common consequences of denying grief:

✳ Lots of illness (real and/or imagined)

✳ Depression

✳ School phobia

✳ Marked increase in separation anxiety

✳ Learning difficulties

✳ Regression to an earlier developmental stage

✳ Sleeping problems – for example, nightmares, restless nights

✳ Eating problems

✳ Bed-wetting

✳ Inability to concentrate

✳ A flatness or lethargy

✳ Anger, violence or rage

✳ Manic behaviour

✳ Deliberate self-isolation

✳ Catastrophising fears of loss of other loved ones

✳ Hyperactivity (some children are diagnosed as hyperactive, but it is just that they are running and running from their confusion and grief)

✳ Some kind of searching

For some children after loss, the pain of grief is so awful they move into a numbness that is deadening: 'When my mother died, I felt nothing. But it was a very spooky nothing' (Dinnage, 1990, p169).

Children may deaden themselves as a defence against grief when their feelings are just too strong and painful and, for whatever reason, they do not or cannot find a comforting adult to help them mourn. Defending against grief means you do not have to feel the whole host of intensely painful, complex, disturbing feelings involved in grieving an awful loss or separation. The problem is, however, that unmourned grief can become like a build-up of silt inside, which deadens, stifles and suffocates too much of the child's feeling life, sometimes causing actual emotional developmental arrest. As a result, the child can all too easily lose his appetite for life.

Numbing against grieving can result in any of the following for the child:

✳ Not letting himself register the fact that this person mattered *deeply* to him.

✳ Not letting himself register the *full* shock of it, the *full* impact of it, the depth of his pain – diminishing its impact on him. Jamie, aged eight, who loved his mother deeply, said after her death: 'Well, we all have to die sometime.'

✳ Just feeling numb after it happened. (This is the natural first stage of any mourning process, but the child may have got stuck in it.)

✳ Feeling detached from the whole thing. Healthy detachment is the final phase of the mourning process, in the sense of readiness to *let go* of the loss and move on. But if the pain of grief has been unbearable, or if *fear* of the pain of grief feels too frightening, the child may have tried to skip all the other phases of the grieving process – the agony, despair, anger, yearning, etc – and jumped straight into a state of totally premature detachment.

✳ Bowlby, the psychoanalyst, wrote in 1988 of various studies – James Robertson (1953), Christoph Heinicke and Ilse Westheimer (1965) – in which children between the ages of one and three, when looked after for too long by 'strange people in a strange place … with no one person to act as a mother-substitute', come in time to act as if neither mothering nor contact with humans have much significance. As his caretakers come and go he ceases to attach himself to anyone, and after his return home stays remote from his parents for days, and perhaps for much longer if he is treated unsympathetically (Bowlby, 1988, p54).

✳ The problem with emotional numbing is that it can actually deaden, so much that the child, in important ways, is no longer open to life.

Grieving children who move into a life of searching, longing and yearning

Dennis Nilsen, aged six, grieving for his dead grandfather:

> On the rocks I stood gazing at the all-powerful restless sea... I would stand for some time with a tear-filled face looking out there for [Grandpa] to come and comfort me as he had always done ... So I sought the silent lonely places where he had taken me, and prayed to my silent god on the horizon of the sea. (Masters, 1985)

A child who has lost a loved one may move into all kinds of symbolic and displaced searching activities. With younger children who have lost a loved one, the loss of their doll or a little car can seem like a tragedy, and may elicit all manner of manic and desperate searching activities, with desperate bouts of crying. The 'searching' for the lost loved one has unconsciously become transferred to material objects. Other children do not displace their feelings in this way. They stay with the longing and the yearning.

> **Terry, aged eight**
> Terry was eight, and his mother had died. At school, he kept watching the door. When asked why, he said, 'In case my Mummy comes back from heaven and walks into the room again.' He knew about the finality of death, and yet the strength of his desperate hope and longing meant he could not let go of her.

Other children, when helped, can speak so movingly about how they long for a cuddle from the very person they have lost; how they long to touch her hair again, take her hand, tell her about what happened to them at school today. For these children, the pain of the absence is awful. They can find it so difficult to think of anything except the person who has left.

The urge to search for a lost loved one is indeed genetically ingrained in us. Animals who lose a parent also begin searching. In studies of infant monkeys separated from their mothers, they initially search frantically and make distress calls, but eventually become passive.

> During the second year of life there is no lack of records of children left in hospital or nursery watching the door through which a parent has departed, and doing so persistently for several days in the evident hope of seeing him or her return through it. (Bowlby, 1978, p435)

> When Demeter found her daughter had gone [to the Underworld], she neglected the plants and trees to search for her. Without her care, the harvests failed and everything withered and died [ie, winter]. (Evans & Millard, 1995, p11)

Figure 7 'Why do the wolves howl? I think they are howling for their mothers.' (Toby, aged seven.)

Separation anxiety and school phobias – when a child loses a parent, how they can be terrified of losing the other

Julie, aged seven

Julie's father had died when she was six, and she was now terrified of her mother dying: 'Something awful might happen to her in our time apart, so I'm so scared I'll never see her again.'

This separation anxiety is a typical response for a child who has lost one parent and naturally fears losing the other. In the child preoccupied with fantasies of catastrophic loss (as a result of what has happened to him), school phobias are not in fact phobias about school but rather a terror of separation from the remaining parent. Separation anxiety can lead to morbid preoccupations that the remaining parent will die in a car crash, or get kidnapped, murdered, etc, and that they will never be reunited. This fear of no reunion is fuelled by the fact that when the loved one died there *was* no reunion.

Pippa, aged five

Pippa, aged five, whose Daddy had died when she was three, was beside herself when her mother went out of the house without her. She was sure that this was the last time she would see her Mummy. She would move all her books in front of the front door in an attempt to barricade her mother in the house! Pippa was also terrified if Mummy got a common cold (imagined in Pippa's head as the start of a downward slope, which would end with her Mummy dying).

The child who cries on the inside, not on the outside

Comforter, where, where is your comforting? (Hopkins, 1985, p61)

Some children who look as if they are coping too well with the death or permanent departure of a parent are weeping quietly inside. Sometimes these children need to see grieving adults cry, in order to feel able to express their own grief. Children need role models of adults who can weep at loss, to know that it is safe and natural. It is unhelpful for the child who bottles up his feelings to be around adults who are bottling up theirs!

If such a child is to let go, he needs to be with someone with whom he feels very safe; someone he knows intuitively is comfortable with grief – who will not pull away from it, or try to distract him away into happier feelings. As Bowlby (1973) said, 'We can only really mourn in the presence of another.' This is such a true statement for grieving children. The feelings are just too strong to unleash on their own, and besides it is far too lonely. When children like this find someone with whom they feel very safe and trusting, there can be a flood of feelings. These children, who have been stoically avoiding or defending against letting go and crying, find one day that the dam breaks. They start to sob uncontrollably.

The agony of rupture – when the loved one leaves or dies suddenly

Simon, aged eight

Simon was eight, and his father had left: 'I woke up. It was a Sunday. Daddy had left a note saying he was leaving Mummy. I didn't see him again.'

The betrayal, then the abandonment

Figure 8 Sally was 13. Her father hit both her and her mother and then left. He did not return. This is a depiction of Sally's sand play story. See how wounded and abandoned the little figure is. Sally chose a broken doll to represent herself. She said, 'The cockerel attacks the child then leaves.'

It is one thing to have time to say goodbye – to grieve with the person who is dying or leaving. It is quite another thing for there to be no goodbye. Here the child knows the violence of broken connection. Perhaps their loved one died in a car crash; took their own life; or one day just walked out on the family and did not come back.

It is truly a terrible thing if a child is deprived of a goodbye. He is deprived of grieving for the person *while they are still there or alive, while they are still there to listen to their grief*. This can be an immensely healing part of the grieving process – to be able to say all the things you want to say to the dying or leaving loved one, and to listen to what they have to say to you.

Children who have suffered from rupture in this way need quality time with a relative or therapist on a regular basis to deal with the shock. Without this, they can be left with a legacy of post-traumatic shock – sometimes for years, sometimes a lifetime.

For many children, surviving the actual death of a parent can be far easier to cope with than a parent who just walks out one day and never comes back. This is because, in the latter case, a child may be plagued with painful fantasies about that parent enjoying life *without* them, even perhaps remarrying and so enjoying someone else's children. They may find themselves preoccupied with thoughts of the father or mother who left, visiting lovely places, going on holiday with someone else and their children.

The result is not only a terrible grief but a terrible hurt, with all the fantasies of not being wanted, not being loveable enough for them to want to stay and be their parent etc. As Susie Orbach says:

> Accepting the painful finality of death is ultimately what helps people to grieve and so to heal; to start life again without the loved one's presence. In separation, by contrast, the wish to connect or re-attach can be stimulated again and acted upon many times over many years before there is a resolution. (1994, p194)

The child whose parent leaves as a result of divorce or separation and does not return

The agony of a parent leaving – say after a divorce or separation – can feel to the child like personal rejection. It can result in massive confusions and irrational fantasies. For example, 'If I'd been more loveable, Daddy would have stayed with Mummy even if they didn't get on all that well.' Some children live with the fantasy (or reality) that their Mummy or Daddy is giving all the love and delight and specialness that they used to give *them*, to someone else. How can a child possibly bear this thought without help? 'The word abandonment comes from the Old English verb *bannan*, meaning "to summon" (OED) … Abandonment means literally "to be uncalled"' (Woodman, 1985, p34). Children who have lost a parent through separation or divorce, who never returns, are indeed 'uncalled'.

How some children who have suffered loss move into clinging behaviour that can drive people away

Lucy, aged thirteen
Lucy's father had died when she was four.

Ever since Lucy's father died, she had been terrified of losing the people she liked or loved. She became over-compliant with everyone she liked – so much so that she would move into serving them in some way, doing errands for them, giving them her toys, packed lunch etc. As a result, aged 13, she was being used and abused by friends who started to see her as a push-over.

'Abandonment feelings aren't solved by super-glued friendships.'
(Orbach, 1994, p128)

The terrible thing about someone leaving you for good is your lack of control, your impotence. So it is understandable that children will start trying to prevent this from ever happening again. However, it is the very act of control that can make it happen again. Clinging is just a desperate attempt at control – control to keep you near me; control to keep myself as near to you as possible: 'If I close the distance between us as much as possible, then I feel safe.' The problem is that such children do not then take into account the feelings of emotional suffocation of the other. This can lead to them being left all over again.

Unworked-through trauma of loss can mean unconsciously enacting it in some form or other throughout life

Children can be helped to understand the Freudian concept of repetition compulsion. This means we unconsciously keep repeating aspects of our painful past in our present, because they have never been properly thought about, felt about and grieved. Or looked at another way, as we have said, feelings pushed down into the dark basement of the unconscious do not go away, but rather stay on to haunt in some way, with the theme of abandonment and loss being repeated again and again. Here is Freud on the subject:

> The [self] which experienced the trauma passively, now repeats it actively in a weakened version, in the hope of being able itself to direct its course. It is certain that children behave in this fashion towards every distressing impression they receive, by reproducing it in their play. In thus changing from passivity to activity they attempt to master their experiences psychically. (Freud, 1979, p327)

Freud is right. Children lucky enough to have the benefit of play therapy can enact their trauma of loss through play. Others less fortunate are often left to enact their trauma of loss in life (repetition compulsion), often with tragic consequences for self and others. As you will see from the next example, when the trauma of loss is blindly enacted, with no conscious awareness of its meaning, the child can enact what happened to him as either the persecutor or the victim:

Harry, aged eight

Harry's mother walked out on the family when Harry was eight. Harry didn't cry. He repressed his grief and got on with his life. But on reaching adolescence, each time he had a girlfriend, he would suddenly ditch her one day, without warning. When he grew up, he got married, but one day walked out on his wife. Harry then had three more engagements and broke them all off. Eventually, he went into counselling and, for the very first time, grieved about his mother walking out on him. This ended 30 years of enacting his own grief and rage unconsciously (repetition compulsion), this time with women as victims and himself as the perpetrator.

From this example we can see that, for some children whose parent has left or died, loss and love can become inextricably bound together in their mind. This can continue right into adulthood, causing all manner of problems in intimate relationships.

> The traumatic neuroses give a clear indication that a fixation to the moment of the traumatic accident lies at their root. These [people] regularly repeat the traumatic situation in their dreams ... It is as though these [people] had not finished with the traumatic situation, as if they were still faced by it as an immediate task which has not been dealt with ... (Freud, 1991, pp314–5)

Children who have grieved the loss of a loved one who then returns

> When the mother did return it was with the baby. Peggy recalled feeling at this time, 'This was not my mother, it was a different person' (a feeling that we know is not uncommon in young children who have been separated from their mothers for a few weeks). (Bowlby, 1979, p59)

When a parent returns after a child has been in great pain during her absence, the child may have become detached. There is no more running up to her with glee. No smile or hug – just a looking straight through her, as if at a stranger. There is a pattern of response to the lost parent, which we also find in higher primates. It is called *Protest – Despair – Detachment* (Bowlby, 1973, p46). The *protest* is in the intense crying and howling when Mummy leaves the room or, in an older child, a pleading to stay. The child may then go into a period of *despair*. A parent being away for too long can indeed feel like a death to the child. He can move into a state of bereavement – not sleeping, not eating, lying helpless, not wanting to play, desperate bouts of crying, etc. When this becomes just too relentless, with the pain at an unbearable level, *detachment* is the third and final stage. Detachment is a cutting-off, a hardening of the heart. Many tough hardened children are stuck in this.

When the parent returns, her response is critical to mending the rift with her child. Of course, the child may be furious. The sentiment is usually along the lines of 'Your leaving made me feel like I had lost you forever. I was tormented with a terrible pain and anguish about you and yet you, my comforter, were not here to comfort me through it.' (With some children this fury may not come out in words but in behaviour.) So:

✳ Can the parent bear the child's anger at her?

✳ Is the parent able to understand and empathise with his reaction, rather than move into blind punishment?

✳ Is the parent able to deal with the phase of clinging which often comes after the anger because the child is frightened she will go again?

✳ With older children, is the parent able to listen without impatience or frustration, and bear the child's intense, enraged verbal and physical outbursts about her having gone away?

If, however, the parent does not understand about the painful stages of re-attachment, the child may fail to get the empathic response he needs to be able to repair himself and their relationship. For example, if he is pushed away for clinging too much, criticised for his healthy protesting anger at being left, or met with the cold or indifferent face of the parent when he has been desperately yearning for her, then interactive repair will not happen. As a result, something inside the child may die. He may make an unconscious decision to block all feelings of loss in the future, to harden his heart, to become tough, emotionally closed or even bitter.

Where a parent is unable to deal with, or even see the child's pain and grief in response to her absence, it is sometimes because when she herself was young, her *own* intense feelings, desperate states of need, pain and longing often met emotional blindness from her parents.

Freddie, aged three

Freddie, whose mother had frequently been away in hospital during his short life, developed a very interrupted sleeping pattern on her return. He would wake up several times a night, distraught and crying, *'I've lost my teddy!'; 'I've lost my blanket!'; 'I've lost my truck!'*. They were in fact right by him, and sometimes he was even holding them. He would 'lose them' repeatedly throughout the night, and the same thing would happen. His mother was exhausted, and started to get irritated. She failed him by calling him attention-seeking, rather than trying to understand his underlying feelings towards her, and that something between them desperately needed to be repaired.

The worse plight of infants who have never had anyone to grieve

This is a primal terror: that we have been left, cast aside to fall apart or peter out, before our life could claim to have begun. (Herman, 1987, p73)

In his book *Touching* (1971, p98), Ashley Montagu provides alarming statistics regarding orphanage babies who were 'fed and watered' but not given any loving attention. In each case he cites, all the babies died. He also cites the case of one orphanage with a very friendly old woman worker who would carry a sick baby around with her on her hip. Although medically very sick, 'old Anna's' babies always survived. This shows how dependent babies are on some loving contact in order to survive. It is a complete myth that food, water and warmth alone will keep a baby alive.

Many babies who have never been loved do indeed stop wanting to live. They are in a state of terrible defeat. Some no longer want to eat anything and so have to be drip-fed because of this dangerous state of withdrawal. Their bodies go limp. There is a frightening deadness in their eyes. They have given up. There is no healthy protest, no calling for help, or comfort in crying.

The vital role of comfort for one's very survival was also researched by Harlow with monkeys. Scientific research (Harlow & Mears, 1979) found that baby monkeys separated from their mothers and given a choice of an artificial 'cloth' mother or a 'wire' mother who offers food down a tube, will choose the comfort of the cloth mother over the food mother.

UNDERSTANDING WHY LOSS IS SO PAINFUL

Understanding the psychology of attachment

Attachment behaviour simply means the natural human drive to attach deeply to another human being, to form a very significant, emotional bond. This is totally healthy and natural, not pathological or regressive. In fact, whether we like it or not, we are genetically programmed to need and form primary attachments – attachments that are deeply significant to us, and which give our life meaning and richness.

The mistake is to think that attachment behaviour is simply something belonging to childhood: it is not. It continues throughout life. However, primary attachments to more than a few individuals would be impossible, as we have only limited reserves of emotional energy. That is how we are made. You can really *like* a lot of people, and indeed be very fond of them, but you will have primary attachment bonds to just a few of them. The main founder of attachment theory explains that, 'Attachment behaviour is directed towards one or a few specific individuals, usually in clear order of preference' (Bowlby, 1979, p130).

So how do you know if you have a primary attachment with someone or not? When you are 'attached' to someone, as opposed to just very fond of them, there are *always* intense emotions and intense hormonal reactions involved. These are particularly intense during the forming of a primary attachment (for example, a parent getting to know their baby, and vice versa) and during the deepening and strengthening of the attachment (for example, being in intimate conversation – verbal or nonverbal – or being in physical contact). One main feature of a primary attachment is that in periods apart, you really miss your loved one, to the extent that it is painful at times, and you want to seek them out and re-establish the bond. This differentiates good friends, whom you really like, but whom you do not miss strongly in this way when you don't see them for a while. Another sign is if the attachment figure leaves or dies. The pain is terrible. There is no escaping it. Whereas if a friend who was not a primary attachment figure dies, you can feel very sad, but you are unlikely to be the one in floods of tears at the funeral and in agony for months afterwards because your whole world feels as if it has been blown apart. Your sadness with the loss of a friend, as opposed to an attachment figure, can of course be painful, but it will not move into an unbearable emotional pain.

For a child, when his primary attachment bond to someone is strong, secure and unthreatened, then being attached can be the source of the greatest joy. It provides essential meaning to his world, brings colour, light, and inner wealth and abundance to his life. It gives him real psychological strength, and sustains his hope when he is in the most challenging of external circumstances. It can make him feel fundamentally safe in the world. A life lived with strong attachment bonds will enable him to perceive the world as fascinating. Its beauty will not only be seen, but deeply experienced. A love of the person is transferred to a love of life:

> The process of [transferring] love from a person to a love of life is of the greatest importance for the development of the personality and of human relationships: indeed one may say, for the development of culture and civilisation as a whole. (Klein, 1988c, p268)

For a child with secure, deeply loving attachments, even if he loses this sense of an awesome beautiful world from time to time, he will reconnect with it before very long. As Reid says, '[his primary attachment] acts as an "internal support" when he is exposed to the ugliness in the world and in himself' (Reid, 1990, p48). Furthermore, a strong, secure attachment bond also provides the child with a secure base in the world from which he will want to get out there and explore, to get a hold on life and live it.

Why is this? What is this attachment relationship doing to the child's body and brain? We will look at that now.

Understanding the biochemistry of love, in order to understand the biochemistry of loss

Primary attachments are rooted in certain brain and body chemistries. When an attachment bond between two people is deeply loving, then at times of intimacy – shared delightful play states, when comforting distress, or moments of real emotional connection – the brain's emotion chemicals and the body's hormones, which are released in both people, feel exquisite. When flowing strongly, it is these chemicals and hormones that make a child or adult feel warm and tender, deeply content, and that all is well in their world. This is far more than just a state of calm that you might get from looking at the sea, for example. It is a far richer response, and results in feeling expansive, potent and very loved.

These powerful natural chemicals, released in lovely interactions with a deeply loved person, are called oxytocin and opioids. Research has shown that both animals and humans prefer to spend more time with those in whose presence they have consistently experienced oxytocin and opioids. As Panksepp, a neurobiologist, says, 'We can infer from work with animals that brain oxytocin, opioids … systems appear to be the key participants in these subtle feelings that we humans call acceptance, nurturance and love … warmth' (1998, p249). Panksepp says these neuro-chemical systems are nature's gifts to us.

Picture an adult and child who get along fine, but are not particularly close. With them, the mood- and behaviour-altering chemicals described above are not strongly activated in their brains and bodies. As a result, their interactions are indeed relatively shallow, and without emotional intensity. In other words, it is the oxytocin and opioids, when strongly activated, that give the powerfully positive emotional intensity to an interaction – that delicious warm quality that makes you glow with the loveliest feeling. The following adult–child interactions strongly activate the release of oxytocin and opioids:

* Tenderly holding a child

* Comforting their distress (particularly with physical holding)

* Helping them regulate their feelings and bodily arousal

* Rough-and-tumble play

* Listening to a child's problems and pain

* Entering into their imaginative play, sitting on the floor with them and showing real interest, particularly if this involves touch.

If a child has a parent with whom he consistently enjoys these interactions, then even when the parent is not there, opioids will be activated just by thinking of that parent. This is why the transitional object is so powerful (the old blanket, etc), because it smells or feels like the soft parent's body. Once the child holds it, opioids will be activated.

We know from animal research that socially satisfied mammals (animals and humans) do not want to fight (Panksepp, 1998, p257). 'Socially satisfied' means that the body-mind is strongly activating oxytocin and opioids on a regular basis. So children who have lots of loving interactions, delightful playful interactions with their parents and the consistent comforting of distress states, tend to be far less aggressive than a child who has not been treated in this way. We also know from animal studies that oxytocin injected into the brain reduces all forms of aggression (Panksepp, 1998, p257).

What happens to the brain chemistry of children who lose someone they love deeply?

> We simply feel normal and comfortable when we are in the midst of friendly company and that same feeling becomes warmer when we are among those we love deeply ... When this feeling of normalcy is suddenly disrupted by the undesired loss ... or the unexpected death of a loved one, we find ourselves plunged into one of the deepest and most troubling emotional pains of which we, as social creatures are capable ... The psychic pain informs us of the importance of those we have lost. (Panksepp, 1998, p260)

When a child loses someone he loved deeply, the wonderful hormones and brain chemicals described above are no longer dominant in his brain, and other very painful chemicals can take over. This results in acute psychological pain for a child or an adult. Hence the child who loved someone deeply will suffer terribly if that person dies or leaves. There is no getting away from this – it is how the human brain and body are genetically programmed. We can see this all too easily in the desperate crying of a baby when Mummy walks out of the room: the baby goes through a mini bereavement process each time this happens. He has no way of knowing that the present isn't forever.

Separation distress triggers incredibly strong stress hormones which the infant cannot possibly manage all alone. So separation distress is hormonal hell. The separation distress circuit in the brain is connected to one of the pain systems in the brain. This is located in the Periaqueductal Gray (PAG), a neuroanatomical structure set deep within the brain (see Figure 9). In other words, the chemistries of pain in the brain are actually linked to the chemistries of separation distress, hence the grieving child or adult is in psychological pain. It is all too common for adults not to appreciate this. You can't just say to a toddler who is crying for his mother because she has just left the room, 'Look, try not to feel this.' Yet many people give that sort of

 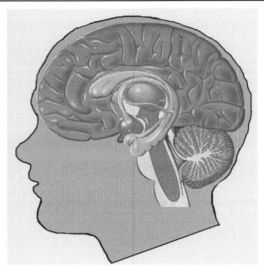

The chemistries of pain in the brain are linked to chemistries of separation distress

Pain circuit deep within the reptilian part of the brain

The linking of the pain systems and the separation distress systems deep within the brain. The separation distress circuit in the brain is connected to one of the pain systems in the brain – they share the same brain chemistries and are anatomically overlapping deep in the reptilian part of our brain.

Figure 9 'The language of loss is the language of pain' (Panksepp, 2002, Personal Communication)

message to both the grieving child and the infant screaming for his mother. Many adults utterly underestimate the power of the hormonal hell of both grieving and separation distress.

In addition, the natural brain opioids released when a child deeply loves a parent are actually addictive. As Panksepp says, 'Social bonds are to some extent mediated by opioid-based, naturally occurring addictive processes within the brain' (1998, p255). Panksepp makes the point that losing a loved one is as painful and as powerful as coming off heroin. (Heroin activates the opioid system in our brain or, looked at vice versa, opioids mimic the action of heroin in our brain.) We are all familiar with films of people coming off such drugs – the agony, the torment. The same emotions are experienced by the child who has lost a loved one. So if children are not to be psychologically scarred by this torment, they need help with their feelings, as we shall see in the following section.

Helping a child after the opioid withdrawal in their brain

When a child loses someone he has loved deeply – someone who consistently activated natural opioids in his brain – he can be left in a state of opioid withdrawal. To make matters worse, this shift in biochemistry can activate opposing chemical forces in the brain. This involves the release of too high levels of a chemical called acetycholine, which washes very strongly over the higher brain and can make us feel very angry or hostile. It is the same with other mammals – for example, higher primates like chimpanzees, who are accustomed to high levels of opioids. When these are no longer strongly activated in their brains, these animals become very nasty with each other.

Figure 10 From grief to anger. Losing a loved one, can mean a withdrawal of natural calming opioids in the brain, particularly if there is no one in the child's life to whom he wants to turn for comfort. The withdrawal of opoids releases opposing forces – namely a brain chemical called acetycholine. This is released in too high quantities. As a result, it can make both children and adults very angry or hostile. Acetycholine will return to base rate if the child is both comforted and accepts that comfort.

Figure 11 The physical comforting of a grieving child, will release natural calming opioids in the brain, coupled with the lovely emotion chemical, oxytocin. These will block the toxic chemistry of too high levels of acetycholine (which can all too easily move a grieving child into anger). This is why it is vital for children who are suffering from loss to receive comfort. 'Both opioids and oxytocin are powerful anti-aggressive molecules, and they also have a powerful inhibitory effect on separation distress' (Panksepp, 1998, p257).

It is only if this 'potentially or actually aggressive child' receives comfort for his grief that he will feel calmed. The comforting of grief – particularly physical comforting – will once again release opioids and oxytocin in the child's brain. These block this toxic chemistry of too high levels of acetycholine. This is why it is vital for children who are suffering from loss, and who have moved into aggression, to receive high-quality comfort (see Figure 11).

So it is not hard to see that if a grieving child has no person to whom he wishes to turn as a source of comfort, then he has no psychobiochemical brakes on the aggressive behaviour that can be the natural biochemical legacy of his grief. We also know that children from violent backgrounds with insufficient comforting of distress, or help with difficult feelings, show low serotonin in their blood (Kotulak, 1997). Monkeys who have low serotonin are impulsive and aggressive. 'Given the opportunity, they will make dangerous leaps from tree to tree that other monkeys won't attempt. They get into frequent fights.' (Kotulak, 1997, p85)

In terms of these biochemical facts, the following statistics are not at all surprising:

✳ Seventy per cent of men in prison suffered a broken attachment in childhood (National Association for the Care and Rehabilitation of Offenders statistic).

✳ The biggest group of children who are excluded from school for bad behaviour before the age of nine are the group who have suffered a bereavement (Home Office Statistics, 2001).

✳ About half of all bereaved children develop problems of behaviour in the year following the death [of a parent] (Fristad *et al*, 1993).

What a tragedy that many of the children detailed in the statistics above will have had no therapist, counsellor or other attachment figure who could comfort them, and in so doing change their brain biochemistry from too high levels of acetycholine and too low levels of serotonin, back to the activation of levels of opioids, oxytocin and serotonin sufficient for them to move into a place of calm. It also becomes imperative for us to be acutely aware of a child who has lost a loved one, and whether or not he has another person in his life to whom he can turn, *and wishes to turn*, for solace and comfort. If not, it is vital to ensure he gets help before he habituates into states of aggression or violence.

In the light of the above, a highly controversial illustration is the case of the notorious serial killer, Dennis Nilsen. Although many complex factors combine to create a serial killer, a contributory factor can often be traced to a broken attachment at an early age. Nilsen's grandfather (not his mother) was his primary attachment figure. The event of his grandfather's death distorted Nilsen's personality for life. When as an adult he killed men, he would then cuddle up to their dead bodies in bed (for soothing, not sex), and put them in armchairs and talk to them. As a child, Dennis had been given no help whatsoever with his grief about his grandfather. It was a terrible grief, as he had loved him very deeply. When his grandfather died, Dennis purportedly tried to kill himself. (This is interesting in terms of Jane Goodall's research, 1990, in which, as we have seen, she found that many young chimps do not survive the death of their mother. Although they are physically able to support themselves, they just give up and die.)

The horror of Dennis's adulthood is a very sobering lesson about the knock-on effects of leaving a child with a terrible grief, *and with no means of coping with that terrible grief*. Masters writes movingly about Nilsen as a grieving child:

> Someone told him to be a 'big man'. He did not weep. For a long time afterwards, no one so much as mentioned [his dead grandfather's] name. It was as if he had evaporated. The six-year-old boy was not told that he was dead ... It was months before Dennis finally realised that this time there would be no home-coming, and his retrospective grief was so painful that he submerged it and refused to acknowledge its cause. Now ... he

> attributes the seed of his disordered personality to the numbing experience of seeing his grandfather asleep for the last time, the light of his life taken from him. (Masters, 1985, p49)

> At about eight years old, Nilsen attempted suicide in the sea. He looks back on the event and says: 'Many years ago I was a boy drowning in the sea. I am always drowning in the sea ... down amongst the dead men, deep down. There is peace in the sea. (Masters, 1985, p51)

Nilsen's grandfather had worked at sea. The suicide attempt in the sea could be seen as a final attempt to be reunited with his grandfather. There are many stories that act out such an impulse to be reunited in death: *Swan Lake* and *Romeo and Juliet* are just two of the most famous.

Nilsen reflects most poignantly on his lack of help as a child with his bereavement: 'Self-knowledge arrived too late to save the dead or myself ... misplaced love out of its time and out of its mind.' (Masters, 1985, p18)

Nilsen then goes on to talk about the comforting of grief. He did not know about the biochemistry of comfort, and yet he seems to know it intuitively in making the following statement: 'It must be the most wonderful gift to be able to throw your arms around someone and just weep.' He knew exactly what he would have needed to prevent the terrible chemical imbalance being established in his brain which led him, in part, to such appalling violence. 'I have gone a million miles beyond the pale and in the depths of my space I can't even hear myself scream' (Nilsen cited by Masters, 1985, p303).

Nilsen is a horrific reminder of how things can go terribly wrong for the grieving child who is left uncomforted. His biographer is eloquent on this point, 'If he were merely a monster we could learn nothing by studying his deplorable behaviour; it is because he is also human that we must make the attempt' (Masters, 1985, p280).

This connection between uncomforted grief and violence is worryingly not yet well-established knowledge for teachers, parents and child professionals.

Simon, aged six

Simon's father died when he was five, and his mother was very depressed. After the death of his father, Simon had been excluded from school several times in the last year for violent behaviour.

In therapy:

Simon: The dinosaur is fighting. It is fighting because it is too hungry.

Therapist: Yes, when your heart is hungry, not your tummy, it can make you feel desperate with too much fighting inside you. It is just too painful for any child to have to feel.

Simon starts to cry for the first time since his father died.

Parent–child relations which are too weak, and the brain biochemistry of a child who does not need to grieve

So what happens to the grieving process of a child who has not experienced these powerful opioid and oxytocin inducing interactions with a parent? What happens to the child who has had a somewhat distanced, over formal or detached relationship with his parent? In short, if that parent dies or leaves the child will not be in an acutely painful state of opioid withdrawal. Such a child will be spared the pain, but also in effect he has missed out on some of nature's most wonderful gifts.

When a parent, for example, is not good at touch, cuddles, physical play, taking the time to listen to the child, or comforting distress, then the emotional connection between parent and child will be weaker, biochemically speaking. If this is the case, the child will not have experienced the blissful feeling of profound contentment, of calm, of true expansiveness from being in deep connection with a loving other. He is highly unlikely to know that he is missing out on so much. His life is just the way it is.

Although he has never been in love with this parent, perhaps the child has shared some good times with his parent, when he felt interested, curious or excited. For these feelings, your brain needs a cascade of a chemical called dopamine. But this chemical is not important in bonding (Panksepp, 1998, p260). It is only opioids and oxytocin that are involved in the chemistry of bonding. (You can activate dopamine strongly by all manner of activities – eating, drinking, skiing, fairgrounds, satisfying work, etc.)

Charlie, aged twelve

Charlie's father died when he was 12. His teachers were worried because he did not grieve. They did not realize that Charlie had never been close to his father.

Charlie had always wanted to play on the computer during playtime. He saw no reason to have friends, although he was very civil with people who talked to him. Charlie's parents were also more at ease relating to technology than to people. When Charlie's mother came into school, she said, 'We didn't really understand about babies and Charlie didn't cry much. He was happy, I think, to be left in a room in his cot looking up at his mobile. We fed and watered him. We often took him out with us to cafés and posh restaurants. He was no trouble, he seemed content to lie in his cot, while we talked to each other or read the newspaper. My husband and I played with him when we had time, but neither of us are into touch and cuddles. Our own parents weren't good with all that touchy stuff or playing stuff.'

Charlie was neither autistic nor suffering from Asperger's Syndrome. He had just never experienced the wonderful and very particular hormonal release you get from a strong attachment relationship. So he had no desire to have such relationships, and his lack of grief for his father was a biochemical reality.

Charlie seemed happy enough (dopamine release from interacting with his computer), although computer games etc, can never bring the feeling of intense aliveness and deep fulfillment that can be achieved through attachment to someone who can respond to you *on an emotional level.*

An adult I worked with, who had a similar childhood background to Charlie, did not cry when both of her parents died when she was in her twenties. People called her hard-hearted. I did not share this view. My client simply had never really 'met' her parents, emotionally speaking. This is shocking for some people to realise, who accuse such children and adults of just denying their grief. We should be careful before making such judgements, and rather enquire whether the child had a secure and powerful attachment to his parents in the first place. In my client's case, her connection with both parents in childhood was too weak to have ever activated high levels of bonding chemicals. My client described herself and her parents in her childhood as three planets in the sky: 'They co-exist there, but that's about it.'

It is by no means automatic that a child forms a strong attachment to a parent. If a child is not talked to enough, comforted, listened to, cuddled enough (or at all), then opioids and oxytocin will not be strongly activated in the brain. As a result, no strong attachment will form. Most poignantly, in the film *Nil by Mouth*, the main character who was beaten repeatedly as a child by his father said, 'My father thought the word father was enough. It wasn't.' Blood relations is not what it is about. It is about interactions.

Therefore, in considering whether a child is blocking his grief or genuinely does not need to grieve, one needs to ask the question: 'Were there enough lovely interactions between parent and child to engender love – interactions that had a profound effect, on a psychobiochemical level, on the child's developing brain?' Mitchell (1988) calls these 'crucial exchanges'; Stern (1993) calls them 'now moments'. These are moments of real comfort or compassion, or shared times of delight, laughter and interactive physical play. If there have been too few of these, or none, the child has too little to grieve, in the sense that he has not really lost anything of great value. This concept is often difficult for people to accept. They immediately move into 'I am so sorry' to the child, without finding out first whether that child did in fact deeply love his Daddy or his Mummy.

On a final note, when children like Charlie reach adolescence or adulthood, their relationships with objects often wear thin. They start to get less and less pleasure from them. The objects – fast car, computer games, etc – can no longer protect them from a growing sense of futility and meaninglessness about their life. On a biochemical level this is true. As we have seen, exciting relationships with objects release a chemical called dopamine. But the more familiar you are with the object, the more daily contact, the less dopamine will be released in your brain in response to it. Hence the phenomenon of adults always needing to buy that new car, new computer, etc – to get that delicious dopamine boost in their brain all over again. This fading biochemistry does not happen with attachment relationships. The chemical release of opioids and oxytocin will stay just as strong, when you love someone deeply – in fact, it will get stronger and stronger, the more interactions and strong emotional connections you have.

The complex issue of losing a parent who was sometimes loving and sometimes cruel

Some children who have been both abused and loved by a parent who then leaves or dies, grieve them bitterly. This is because, despite the bad times, there were sufficient times of lovely crucial exchanges to excite both hope and love in the child. These times would have activated the release of opioids and oxytocin in the child's brain. Hence, despite the abuse or neglect, these children are not spared the painful state of opioid withdrawal described previously, when they lose this parent. In fact the abused child can miss dreadfully the parent who has been cruel to him, sometimes all the more so because of the on-off treatment. We know from experiments with rats and peanuts, that the rat who was given only the occasional nut from a tube became addicted to the tube. They would not move away from it, in the hope of a nut. Rats given lots of nuts (equivalent to lots of love) or no nuts (equivalent to no love) could easily move away from the tube. Addiction is set up very effectively by intermittent reinforcement in this way.

This is not to say that some children who have been both loved and abused do not cut off from their grief if they lose the abusing parent. This is because of the level of their rage and hurt. Their sense of betrayal can block their loving feelings. The child can then cut off from his feelings of grief and move into a defensive position of 'I don't care that he's dead. Good riddance to bad rubbish.' (Hence the child who becomes hardened and tough.) The death or loss of the parent is experienced as just one more betrayal, just one more hurt, just one more abandonment. However, as this child has sometimes been loved and comforted in the ways here described, he cannot ultimately escape the biochemistry of pain after loss. He may later fall into a depression and not link it in any way with the death that he is so desperately defending himself from feeling anything about. Furthermore, it can result in the child cutting himself off from his loving, gentle emotional responsiveness to other people and to life per se. This means he has a narrower range of feelings and so a narrower experience of life. Thus for children who have been both abused and loved, the mourning process can be full of pain and anguish. Such children often need much help to look behind their rage and hurt to their grief.

Finally, however, as we have seen, if a child has been abused and neglected and there has been no comfort and love, he has nothing to grieve. In terms of biochemistry, interactions with this parent will not have activated opioids and oxytocin in his brain. (See page 37.)

HOW TO HELP A CHILD WITH FEELINGS OF LOSS

> It is not possible to fully grieve without the presence of another.
> (Bowlby, 1973)

Staying with a child's feelings, however painful, without moving into platitudes or giving advice

If the child is finding it difficult to speak literally, enable him to speak in images and metaphors. See the exercises in the next chapter, which are designed to be non-threatening for the child suffering from loss. Advice and platitudes, for some grieving children, will block any desire they had to speak about their loss.

Finding words and concepts that are age-appropriate for the child and his concept of death

By and large, children of school age can understand very well about the finality of death. They can understand that the loss is a permanent one, that the loved person will not be coming back. However, little children under the age of five may believe that Daddy or Mummy has just gone to another place – for example, a cloud in the sky, heaven – and is hanging about 'up there'. They may therefore believe that death could be in some way reversible, that Daddy who died will come back some day. Other under-fives are well aware that he will not. It is good to explain to little children what death means. They can often understand things like: 'His body stopped working. When that happens the person dies. No one can keep living without their body.'

Young children often believe, or want to believe, that their loved one, although dead, still has all the senses of an alive person, and can still see, hear, smell, move, etc. It can be very difficult for a young child to conceive of their dead parent as no longer being a sensate being and, even worse, no longer having a brain to think about them, or eyes to see them, or ears to hear them. Little six-year-old James in our earlier example suddenly realised this when he said one day, 'My Daddy can't see my legs any more.' This can be a deeply painful realisation for a child.

Interestingly, for the most part, little children are fascinated by seeing a dead bird on the pavement, or a dead worm. This can be a good time to explain death and the 'body not working' concept.

The importance of not protecting a child from the fact that his parent is dying

By protecting a child from the fact that his parent is dying, you are depriving him of the time left (often preciously short) to say goodbye, and to say all he needs to say to the parent while that parent can still hear and respond. These final crucial exchanges are often vital in easing the mourning process, and can be kept as a wonderful treasure of memories in the child's mind forever. When loving conversations are recalled, natural opioids can be released in the child's mind, just as when the parent was actually with him.

Why attending the funeral can be so healing for a child

Similarly, 'protecting' a child from the funeral is another potential deprivation of a vital method of closure. Adults who deeply loved someone who has died would usually not miss the funeral for anything. It is a vital ending process. So depriving children of this 'in case it upsets them' is folly. They are already deeply upset. Children desperately need models of how to grieve, and how it is natural to cry when you lose someone you love. Seeing how people are at a funeral can serve to normalise their own grief, their own wish to cry and cry.

Furthermore, without going to the funeral or seeing the dead body, children can believe that their parent is still alive somewhere and has just left for a while, and will be coming back. As we have seen, a most horrific and tragic case of this was Dennis Nilsen, the mass murderer, who for many years as a child was not at all clear about the finality of his grandfather's death. No-one spoke of it as a finality, just as a 'sleeping' (see Masters' superb book on this, *Killing for Company*, 1985). In short, without a funeral, the death can feel to the child more like a disappearance or abandonment than a death, with all the difficult feelings this can engender.

Be empathic about the child's fantasies of reunion with the dead person

The child will often talk about being reunited. One little four-year-old boy whose Daddy died when he was two said, 'I would like to die so I can be with Daddy.' A child's wish to kill himself in order to be reunited with a dead person can be shocking to adults, but, for the most part, the wish exists in the world of fantasy, and so is not in danger of being acted out in reality. (If you are worried, see the section on recognising clinical depression in a bereaved child, page 46.)

A child protecting the parent, or a parent protecting the child from grief: why it is unhelpful both ways

Some children pick up that their parent is feeling psychologically over-burdened with grief. So the child decides that there is no space for him to have his grief as well. In fact, he may have fantasies that if he were to cry as well, the parent would break down even more or fall apart completely. Certainly such a child has no faith or hope whatsoever in being comforted.

Sometimes the child is spot-on in this appraisal of his bereaved parent being so fragile and vulnerable. Other times he is way off – he is projecting on to his parent his own feelings that he might fall apart completely if he let himself cry. In such cases, his protection is not helping anyone, especially himself. Such a child needs his parent to open up the subject, to show him she is emotionally strong enough to talk about the death.

However, where a parent is unable to cope with the child's grief as well as her own, she needs to accept this fact without self-blame. She needs to accept her lack of emotional availability at this time, and so should seek out a child counsellor, child therapist, or significant relative with whom her child can work through his grief.

Sometimes the boot is on the other foot. The parent tries to protect the child by not talking about the person who has died or gone. This parent is actually only protecting herself. Nobody talking about the loss can actually inhibit the child's mourning process, or put the brakes on it. There should be photographs around the house; they should not be put away. Of course, if a parent is in deep distress in terms of loud wailing and howling, then a child may feel very frightened by the intensity of this. But a parent shedding tears, etc, is a real model of how to express feelings and the importance of not bottling them up.

Be aware that bereaved children may regress to an earlier age developmentally

Having graduated to a more independent stage, the grieving child may start bed-wetting or soiling, losing speech, losing other educational abilities, or becoming clingy again. It is vital not to punish him for this, but rather to understand that his natural developmental stage (which he may had achieved long ago), of moving from dependency to more independence, can be severly knocked by the painful loss. He has lost a lot of trust. A move back to being a more dependent child may be an attempt at building up enough security in human relationships again to be able to feel free enough to move on once more into independence.

How to help a child whose tragic loss has coloured his entire perception of the world with catastrophising and fears of abandonment

If a child has suffered a terrible loss, he may well be plagued by all sorts of irrational theories that something awful might happen at any moment. In other words his past is completely colouring both his present and his fear of the future. This is a terribly painful way to live life – as the poet Les Murray says, 'The blow that never falls batters you stupid' (1997, p19). Children like this can be helped enormously by information about how the mind works; how past experience can indeed colour their perception of the present; and how the fear circuit in the lower brain (subcortex) can become trigger-happy and react to the future and the present as if it is a repeat of the past. The problem is, the higher brain will not say, 'Hey, you are remembering something.' It will actually make you believe it is about here and now. Without this knowledge about the brain, the child will not be able to test reality, or say to himself, 'Hang on, you are muddling up what happened to you when Mummy died with terrifying fears about the future.'

June, aged thirteen

When she was a little girl, June's father would come home from work, seek out 'his little princess', put her on his knee, and listen to all her stories about her day. Then when she was 10, her father left his wife and went to live abroad with another woman. He did write, but rarely visited. June was heartbroken. It made her totally insecure in all her friendships. Many times she would leave a best friend, thinking they preferred another child to her. She would also reject because she felt so rejected by her father. She felt only pain when boys started to show interest in her. After all, wouldn't any relationship with a male just end in agony? Through adolescent counselling she was helped to see how her inner pictures from her past were superimposing themselves on her perception of her friends now. She was then helped to check her *theory of motivation* about her friends' behaviour. For example, she was convinced that when they did something like look away from her, that meant they were bored and were thinking about leaving her (just like her father had done).

The counsellor helped her to talk to her best friend:

June (aged 13): Mary, when you didn't go ice-skating with me, I thought it was because you didn't want to be my friend any more, is that right?

Mary (aged 13): No, you are completely wrong. Mummy said I had to stay in and help my little brother. I was too embarrassed to tell you. *(Gives June a hug.)*

The hug made June feel really warm and made her realise that her theory of Mary's motivation was wrong, and that she had been muddling up Mary with her father again.

Checking a theory of motivation is a sophisticated action, which lots of adults do not do well! But to deprive children of this skill would be 'childist'. June, and other children like her, can begin to understand that, with a background like theirs, they may well see loss everywhere, or be plagued with persistent fears of loss or abandonment. They may also be vulnerable to clinging behaviour in important relationships, which actually drives the other person away.

> Once the realisation is accepted that even between the closest human beings, infinite distances continue to exist, a wonderful living side by side can grow up, if they succeed in loving the distance between them which makes it possible for each to see the other whole against a wide sky. (Rilke, 1939, p56)

How to recognise when a child suffering from loss has moved into clinical depression and/or suicidal ideation – and what to do

It is important for professionals in childcare, parents and teachers to understand the official diagnostic criteria for depression in children. In terms of the standard psychiatric diagnostic manual used all over the world (*DSM-IV*: American Psychiatric Association, 1994, p327), a major depressive episode is a period of at least two weeks in which there is a 'depressed mood or loss of interest or pleasure in nearly all activities'. In addition, five or more of the following symptoms must be present during that two-week period:

✳ Depressed mood most of the day

✳ Diminished interest or pleasure

✳ Significant gain or loss of weight

✳ Inability to sleep or sleeping too much

Figure 12 'Then he felt the sting of his own sadness. 'I don't want to feel anything ever again,' he said. From the accompanying storybook, *The Day the Sea Went Out and Never Came Back*, Sunderland & Armstrong, 2003.

✳ Bodily agitation or bodily slowing down

✳ Fatigue

✳ Feelings of worthlessness or guilt

✳ Inability to think or concentrate

✳ Thoughts of death or suicide.

I would add the following:

✳ No real interest or curiosity in anything

✳ No capacity to be comforted

✳ Negative feelings and thoughts about self and/or others, life, the future.

If these conditions are present in a child, the situation must be taken very seriously. Suicide accounts for 20 per cent of all deaths in young people. Among those who commit suicide, three in five will have experienced emotional and behavioural difficulties for several months prior to the attempt. Young people who have a friend or relative who has harmed or killed themselves are at greater risk of suicide. A third of adolescents who kill themselves have a history of previous attempts (Mental Health Foundation, 1999; Coleman, 1999).

> **Tony, aged twelve**
> Tony was clinically depressed as a result of being rejected by his mother. His mother could not cope with him, so he was taken into care. He regularly ran away from the children's home, and hid in his mother's garden in order to try to get a glimpse of her at the kitchen window. The next week he threw himself off a high diving board, but not into the swimming pool. Luckily he survived. To him, there was little point in living a life where the love of his life no longer wanted him.

Sometimes a child will disclose his desire to be dead in his stories or play, which can act as a dreadful rehearsal for suicidal acts. As Seneca pointed out: 'The exits are everywhere: each precipice and river, each branch of each tree, every vein in your body will set you free' (cited by Alvarez, 1971, p291). At other times, children will just speak of their suicidal ideation quite overtly. Stella, aged eight, told her teacher one day, 'I think of putting a rope round my neck, but I don't know how.'

Suicide attempts and ideation are beyond the usual brief of teachers or therapists, let alone parents. The child's doctor must always be informed. Depressed children always need an adult in their lives, such as a parent, therapist, relative or teacher who will not tell them to pull themselves together, but who can empathise with what they are feeling, and then find a way of conveying that understanding to them. You cannot just pull yourself together when your entire world has lost its warmth, colour and meaning; when without your loved one everything has gone bleak, cold and hostile. Children who are bereft, depressed or despairing, need to be encouraged to talk about feelings for which it may be too difficult for them to find a vocabulary. Many adults also struggle with this, particularly if they have not known, *or have not let themselves know*, the agony of losing someone they loved deeply. This is where the child therapist or counsellor comes in. They are trained to find the words, so that the child feels deeply understood. It is this level of empathy that can renew a despairing child's faith in the healing of human connection.

The grieving children who are most susceptible to clinical depression

✳ Children who have suffered a major loss – for example, loss of a loved one, of a country, of self-esteem (eg, through migration), which lead them to feel impotent, humiliated, totally alone and trapped.

> Losses which are threatening have the greatest impact, particularly if they result in humiliation or the feeling of being trapped. (Wolpert, 1999, p52)

✳ Children who are not being helped with the pain of their loss. So they try to adapt to it, but fail to do so, which can result in depression.

❋ Children whose parents are depressed. One study (Wolpert, 1999, p44) showed that children of a depressed parent had a threefold greater risk of having a depression, and the peak age of the first depressive episode ranged from 15 to 25 years.

❋ Children who after their loss have no-one with whom they are emotionally close, and so they have no opportunity to truly confide in someone.

Why children need to know about the normality of the acute pain from losing someone you love — so they feel normal, not 'mad'

> The pain of separation is a human phenomenon ... If human attachment is important to someone, separation will always be difficult. (Clarkson, 1989, p149)

Children need to know that losing someone you love hurts like hell, unless you are defending against it. Schools should help with this as part of the curriculum, but they rarely do. No one can escape the pain of loss at some time in their life.

Terry, aged seven
Terry, whose mother had died last year, came home from school one day and told his Nanny that he had had a great day. When asked why, he said: 'One of my friends – her uncle died.' Terry at last didn't feel odd, different, and too alone in his grief. Something so huge and terrible had happened to him, and yet no-one was talking about it and no other child seemed to understand.

Things that can be helpful for a child to know about loss and grieving

When appropriate, find a way that the child can hear the following statements (the ones relevant to them) about the pain of loss and the importance of mourning. If necessary, translate them into age-appropriate language.

✳ The more you have loved, the more it will hurt when you lose the person you love.

✳ Thousands of years ago, a very wise playwright said, 'We inherit grief just by virtue of being born human' (Euripides, *Electra*, 413BC). He was right. It is a fact of life, it cannot be avoided. Some children never know the pain of loss until they are grown-ups. It is hard for a child to know it. Sometimes it means that a child is wiser about the pain of loss than some adults who have not yet suffered it. Sometimes this can make it difficult for a child to get other adults and other children to really understand properly about the pain. But someone somewhere will. And you will know when you have found a person who really can understand.

✳ It is so sad that you had to know loss so early in your life. Lots of people do not have to face it until they are adults.

✳ It is brave to dare to love, because it hurts so much to lose that love. But when you dare to love, it can make life an amazing place to be.

✳ When you lose someone you have deeply loved, and they are not ever going to come back, there is always a shock and your life is changed for ever. It is changed but not destroyed, although at first it may feel as though it is.

✳ When you lose someone you love, it is perfectly natural to feel anger towards them – 'How dare you leave me!' – just as much as sadness. You are not bad for feeling this. Anger is a part of grief.

✳ Mourning means letting yourself dare to feel the pain about the person who died or left.

✳ Mourning means still giving the person who died or left you a very central place in your mind for a while. But this is so that you can separate from them at *your* pace, rather than having their end done *to you* (which is what it can feel like when someone dies or walks out). Mourning helps you to let go in *your* time, rather than in *their* time.

✳ Mourning is absolutely vital if you are going to get over the person you have lost, so you can go on with your life and live it well.

✳ Mourning is too difficult to do on your own. It is a bit like if you have cut your knee very badly, and it hurts horribly; it is too lonely to be on your own then. Being very very sad and daring to really cry hard about someone you loved is too powerful a thing to do on your own. It is a bit like trying to tackle a fire or a flood of feeling all on your own. So do your mourning with a grown-up you really really trust, and really really like, and who is very kind.

✳ Because the pain of losing someone you love hurts so much, some children and some grown-ups try not to feel it at all – but that causes all sorts of problems. It can be like giving yourself an anaesthetic and therefore numb the pain. You do not feel much grief, but you do not feel much joy either. For some people, numbing their grief means they carry around a kind of heavy feeling all the time. This can feel miserable. By not mourning, you become stuck, like you are locked in your past. It is strange, but in fact the only way to move out of your pain is to move into it.

✳ Although you may be in a huge amount of pain, it can be reassuring to know that it is in fact a stage in a process, and that the pain will go away one day.

✳ Do not try to rush the mourning process. Do it in your time when you have found the right person to grieve with.

What to say to a child who has become locked into searching behaviour

'When people lose someone they love, it is very natural for them to try to find them, to search for them, to look for them even when they know they will never find them again. It is very natural to think you see them in the street, when you know they are never coming back. Have you ever had a searching dream? Have you got horribly upset when you lost a toy or something precious, after you lost the person you loved, and you searched and searched for it? This is your mind's way of trying to search for your lost one, but it can get a bit muddled up with the lost toy.'

What to say to a grieving child about how it can really help to talk about it to someone

'Missing can hurt a lot, just like a broken limb, or a cut knee, and so on. It often hurts too much. You just want the pain to go away. Physical pain needs medicine. But for emotional pain, the best medicine is telling someone you really like and trust all about how much you hurt and, if you are brave enough, to let yourself cry in front of that person.'

Helping children with their irrational guilt that they somehow caused the loss

Children sometimes move into guilt if a person they loved dies. 'If I hadn't shouted at Mummy so much and said I hate her, she would still be alive today.' Children need to be helped to understand that angry words or naughty behaviour cannot hurt someone's body and cause them to die.

Helping children who have lost someone suddenly, unexpectedly, without warning

These children have been deprived of saying goodbye, of saying all the things they wanted to say and also of perhaps Mummy or Daddy having time to make a tape or a video talking to them before they died. It is a terrible rupture.

Adults need to acknowledge what a terrible thing it is, not being able to say goodbye, not to have a powerful goodbye connection in their memory; not to have a chance to be left slowly, gradually, so that the leaving is a *shared* process with the one who is going. With a child like this, you need to talk about these things and about shock and rupture and being sundered apart (in child-friendly language). The child may also be suffering from post-traumatic shock.

TABLE 1: A CHILD'S NATURAL REACTIONS TO THE EXPERIENCE OF LOSING SOMEONE DEEPLY LOVED

Initial stages of numbness, disbelief, denial	Shock – a body blow, and resulting physical symptoms – crying, howling, screaming	Yearning, longing or searching	Feeling haunted by the person they have lost	Mental preoccupation with event of loss	Mental preoccupation with lost person
• Denying the permanency of the situation – 'I will see my Daddy again! He will pick me up again!' • Believing that the loss is not forever. They will come back. 'Daddy's just gone away for a bit.' • Feeling that the person is in some way still with them, that they are still accompanying you through life. • Thinking they hear and see the lost person – a voice in a crowd is his, a face is hers – a car exactly like his, a coat exactly like hers. *'With his whole emotional being, it seems, a bereaved person is fighting fate, trying desperately to turn back the wheel of time and to recapture the happier days that have been suddenly taken from him. So far from facing reality and trying to come to terms with it, a bereaved person is locked in a struggle with the past.'* (Bowlby, 1978, p93)	• The shock can feel like a body blow. You might as well have been shot, in terms of the impact of it. The child may literally feel 'shattered' by it. • The child's bodily response to shock may include loss of appetite, bed-wetting, nightmares, wanting to shake and scream. • The shock of the sudden ending of his life as he has known it. • Some children may go into floods of desperate crying *'Both crying and screaming are, of course, ways [in] which a child commonly attracts and recovers his missing mother, or some other person who may help him find her; and they occur in grief... with the same objective in mind – either consciously or unconsciously.'* Bowlby, 1978, pp89–90) Children lucky enough to be with someone they feel very safe with, after traumatic loss, can release the shock trapped in their body by screaming and shaking. Others, sadly, bottle it up for years. The shock of the traumatic loss, if not physically released at some point, can cause endless bodily and emotional symptoms.	• Saying or calling their name. • An urge to search for them. *'Some bereaved people are conscious of their urge to search, others are not ... Whatever attitude a bereaved person takes towards the urge ... he none the less finds himself impelled to search and, if possible, to recover the person who has gone.'* (Bowlby, 1978, p87) *'I look up at the night sky. Is anything more certain than that in all those vast times and spaces, if I were allowed to search them, I should nowhere find her face, her voice, her touch?'* (Lewis, 1966, p15)	• Finding constant reminders and references to them everywhere. People who have Daddy's name, people who look like Daddy, people who talk like Daddy. This can occur 100 times over: with his car, hat, favourite music, job etc, so the world is perceived as one huge, cruel reminder of Daddy. It can seem that there is no relief from it. • Having comforting night dreams of being with them again, of a reunion; more pain on waking, realising this is not reality.	• Repeated turning over and over in their mind of why the loss happened, trying to make sense of it. 'Daddy didn't want to leave.' • Thinking of ways it could have been prevented. 'If only I'd not been naughty that day.' • A compulsion to go over the details of the actual leaving, again and again, or over the last day the child was with Daddy.	• Much of their thought-time is dominated by the person they lost – the memories, the wishes, the images, the longing. • The child keeps referring to them: 'Daddy can't see my legs any more', etc. • Suddenly, out of the blue, while eating an ice cream or half way through a film, 'Daddy shouldn't have left', 'I haven't got a Daddy any more.' *'Grief ... comes from the frustration of so many impulses that had become habitual. Thought after thought, feeling after feeling, action after action, had H for their object. Now their target is gone. So many roads lead through to H. I set out on one of them. But now there's an impassable frontier-post across it. So many roads once; now so many culs-de-sac.'* (Lewis, 1966, p41)

TABLE 2: THE NATURAL EMOTIONAL ROLLER-COASTER OF LOSS FOR THE BEREAVED CHILD (MOVING IN AND OUT OF THE FOLLOWING STATES)

Feelings of despair – in a young child these tend to come out in symptoms, rather than overtly

Despair is particularly prevalent in children who have no other person to whom they want to turn for comfort. Sometimes the despair is particularly focused on the fact that the very person they need to comfort them is the one who has left them.

Feeling terrible emptiness – living in a world that has lost its colour and beauty

Feeling that the other person took too much with them when they left, sometimes even took away a vital part of them, for example, their hope, their very self, their reason for living, their happiness.

Feelings of anger towards the person who has gone (even if they are dead), and feelings of anger towards the surviving parent or carer

Anger as healthy protest against the trauma of the loss.

Anger at the pain they have been left to feel. Sometimes this can feel very strong, when it triggers feelings of *'How dare Mummy leave me!'* But in order to keep the person who has gone or died as good and undamaged in their mind, they are angry with the surviving parent instead.

Anger from a sense of betrayal – *'I really trusted you'* – can fuel a wish for revenge, but again, because the person is gone, this is usually displaced onto someone else.

Feelings of guilt

Seeing themselves as in some way responsible – *'If only I'd not been naughty that day...'* This often falls into two categories:

a) *'If only I'd done X...'*   b) *'If only I hadn't done X...'*

For example: *'I caused this situation; I made him go away. I was responsible for her death in some way. If only I'd done X I could have prevented it.'*

Feelings of fear

Fears of going mad. Fears of the strength of the wish to be dead. Fear of the heart actually breaking: *'No-one ever told me that grief felt so like fear. I am not afraid, but the sensation is like being afraid.'* (Lewis, 1966, p5)

Fear of further loss, of losing the other parent, sibling, etc

'Something might happen to Mummy while I'm at school, so I hate school, I don't want to go to school any more.' The child is very anxious about further loss, and so can develop separation anxiety – *'If I'm away from them something might happen to them as well. I might lose them as well.'* The fear that there will not be a reunion with the parent/sibling etc who is alive.

TABLE 2: THE NATURAL EMOTIONAL ROLLER-COASTER OF LOSS FOR THE BEREAVED CHILD (continued)

Feelings of loneliness

'The bed's too big, the frying pan's too wide.' (Joni Mitchell, 'Blue').
Acute loneliness can be felt, particularly if the child has no other attachment figure to whom they spontaneously turn for comfort. That ache can feel ever-present, and can be particularly strong in places where the child went with Daddy or Mummy, or during times they do something they used to do together.

Erratic changes of mood states

For example, hope interspersed with hopelessness: from *'Daddy will come back'* or *'I'll meet Daddy again in heaven'* to *'I have lost them for ever'*, often rapidly following on from another. Erratic shifts from sadness to anger and vice versa, for example, taking photos of Daddy to bed with them one night, and tearing the photos up the next day; wanting to remember, then wanting to forget; loving Daddy, then hating him for going.

TABLE 3: HOW TO RECOGNISE WHEN A CHILD'S GRIEVING PROCESS IS GOING WRONG – WHEN IT'S TIME TO THINK ABOUT GETTING PROFESSIONAL HELP

Denial that sticks

Daddy's only gone away for a bit, he will be back.

Stephen, aged six: Stephen's Daddy left for good. But after much time had passed, Stephen still thought Daddy would be back and be re-united with Mummy, even when it was clear to everyone else that Daddy had left for good – (now happily married to someone else and expecting their first baby).

Usually, however, in denial there is still a part of the child that knows the truth – that the person they have lost will not be coming back. However, for a few children, their denial is so complete that they can fully believe in the continued presence of the lost person, and so continue life *as if that person were still around*. Reality cannot be allowed into conscious awareness, for fear that the strength of the grief might overwhelm and send them mad.

'Whereas perhaps half of all bereaved people locate the dead person somewhere appropriate, for example in the grave … a minority locate the dead person somewhere inappropriate, for example within an animal or physical object, or within another person, or within the bereaved him- or herself.' (Bowlby, 1978, p161)

TABLE 3: HOW TO RECOGNISE WHEN A CHILD'S GRIEVING PROCESS IS GOING WRONG (continued)

Numbness that goes on way past the usual thawing-out time

'I don't feel anything about his going away. I've never cried about it.'

(**Note**: This is only applicable when the child really loves their parent. Some children will not naturally feel very much if the connection with the lost parent may have been just too weak, broken, indifferent or abusive etc.)

Some bereaved children are numb for years, others for the rest of their life. Children who have been brought up to 'put their best foot forward', or to think 'big boys don't cry', can suffer from this in particular.

Numbness against threatening feelings of loss in childhood often comes out as depression in later life. This is clear, for example, in someone who has felt life to be meaningless for years, but when asked whether they have ever cried for their dead mother who died when they were a child, (whom they loved deeply) they say 'No'. In some people, however, the defense of numbing works for years, and then suddenly they break down somewhere and cannot stop crying.

Moving prematurely to a position of detachment (defensive detachment)

'So quickly, so quickly, the English stop speaking of grief.' (Byatt, 1995, p419)

'Ah well, best move on now'; 'No point dwelling on the past'; 'I didn't really need Daddy anyway.' Cutting off in this way is particularly prevalent when a child sees their other parent dealing with their loss like this. The price for cutting off on their feeling life so dramatically, denying their anger, grief or despair, is often, again, depression, a feeling of deadness or emptiness. This is because repressing one set of strong feelings tends to adversely affect a person's entire passionate attachment to life.

Yearning for the lost person can be transferred unconsciously on to something or someone else which then may become an obsession

When a child's strength of feeling, and the often relentlessness of yearning, is too unbearable, it can get displaced (totally out of conscious awareness) on to yearning for something else. A common displaced yearning is wanting new things all the time. As soon as one thing is bought, the next thing in the shop window is yearned for; or they may keep yearning for comfort substitutes – for example, chocolate, a drink - *'I'll be all right when I have that.'* But of course nothing can ever satisfy, because what is actually being yearned for is not being faced. The problem is that this process of transferring can itself be very painful, both for the child himself and the people who care for him, who never see the child in a state of satisfaction.

TABLE 3: HOW TO RECOGNISE WHEN A CHILD'S GRIEVING PROCESS IS GOING WRONG *(continued)*
Stuck in anger Some bereaved or rejected children are angry a lot of the time. As a consequence, sometimes they lose friends as well, so they have even more loss to deal with (or not deal with!). Anger is used as protection against the far too unbearable feelings of despair, grief and hurt. Tragically, anger used like this can turn into bitterness and a hardened heart for a lifetime.
Feelings of loss get transferred unconsciously on to something or someone else (sometimes for years) This means a child builds up a whole lot of anxiety about losing things – for example, losing their other parent, toys, etc. The child may develop obsessional checking rituals to see that they have their favourite teddy etc, to *prevent a loss in the future that has already happened in their past.* Losing relatively minor things – for example, losing their dummy or Pokemon – may bring on terrible over-the-top feelings of panic.
Stuck in their relationship life The child stops himself from making new relationships in his outer world, as he is still having a relationship with his lost person in his 'inner world'. He never let go of his loved lost person, and so he never moves on. This loyalty, of course, benefits no one. One little boy who had lost his Daddy was stuck in years of rage and hate at his new stepfather. He kept telling him to go in the rubbish and that he smelt vile. He was so locked in with his dead Daddy, he could not let the love of his new stepfather touch him.
The pits of despair that never end Sometimes this can be fuelled by a belief that they have been left *because they are basically unlovable.* There is no light, not even a chink.
Being unable to love again (which can continue right into adulthood) This happens from a fear that *others* will go away too, and leave the child all over again – so they never risk an intimate relationship again. This is a tragic and often unconscious decision.

Enabling the child to find the language of love

Help the child to speak about what it was like to feel loved and to love this person. Not speaking about this renders the bereaved child emotionally poorer. His love needs a voice, just as much as his pain.

The following are concepts for you to put to the child in *age-appropriate* language. Such concepts may help the child to understand about the very nature of love, and so to appreciate why loss of that love can hurt so much. It can also help him understand that if he has been lucky enough to have had a profound human connection with another person, it will remain like a jewel in his memory for ever, and continue to warm him deeply. You may not actually say any of the following things to the child, but instead they may serve to orientate you in a time when a child does talk about what it meant to feel so loved and in love. The following statements (appropriately selected) may therefore enrich your empathic response to the child:

Why love is so special

* You felt very seen by the person you loved, very known, and loved for who you were.

* When you have deeply loved someone, it is because you felt you could be you with this person, without having to try to be someone else.

* When you told them about your feelings, your happiness and your pain, they always seemed to listen and to understand.

* You never grew tired of being with that person.

* You could play with that person, laugh with them, tell them your deepest secrets, tell them your deepest pain, cry with them, get angry with them.

* When you deeply loved this person, you visited some of the richest vistas possible of human relating.

* Being with this person took you into a whole array of colours, tones and hues of delicious feelings – for example, calm, lively, bubbly, excited, loving, tender, quiet, passionate, fascinated, angry, soothing, still. Your

imagination, your humour, your feelings, your body, were all actively engaged in some way, when you were with this person.

✳ The loved person will probably have brought out something very alive in you.

✳ You will have felt very loved by that person – you could light them up, you were their prince or princess.

> We grieve most when we lose those who have helped us to thrive ...' (Panksepp, 1998, p260)

What psychoanalysts and psychotherapists have said about deep connection with someone bringing an intense sense of meaning to life

> Connection with another always both actualises and expands the self ... (Mitchell, 1998, p277)
>
> I have tried to make clear that one part of ourselves that we cherish is the wealth we have accumulated through our relations to people, for these relations and also the emotions that are bound up with them have become an inner possession. (Klein, 1988a, p340)
>
> A soul mate is someone to whom we feel profoundly connected, as though the communicating and communing that takes place between us were not the product of intentional efforts, but rather a divine grace. This kind of relationship is so important to the soul that many have said there is nothing more precious in life.' (Moore, 1992, p xviii)
>
> Love is not only about relationship, it is also an affair of the soul. Disappointments in love, even betrayals and losses, serve the soul at the very moment they seem in life to be tragedies. (Moore, 1992, p96)
>
> All real living is meeting. (Buber, 1987, p11)

and Plato:

> So ancient is the desire of one another which is implanted in us, reuniting our original nature, making one of two, and healing the state of man. (Plato, 1951, p83)

Why the treasure of lovely memories is so important to the child who has lost a loved one

Again, the following concepts and ideas can be offered to the child in age-appropriate language, or just held in mind as a background for your empathic response to the child as he talks about his lovely memories:

✳ 'If love has not been smothered under resentment, grievances and hatred, but has been firmly established in the mind, trust in other people and belief in one's own goodness are like a rock which withstands the blows of circumstance.' (Klein, 1988b, p341)

✳ The child who has really known love and has deeply loved, grows up to see the world as a place with enough hope and goodness, so that with the support of others, even the most awful situations can be endured.

✳ The child who has been able to 'love in peace' is very fortunate. This means that he has not been frightened of his parents, or anxious that either of them might suddenly stop loving him, or that there was not enough love to go around – for example, a fear that it would all get used up by a sibling or a spouse – or that they would only love him on the condition of him being perfect, good, not angry, etc. So in adulthood, he can also 'love in peace'.

PRACTICAL WAYS OF ENABLING CHILDREN TO SPEAK ABOUT AND WORK THROUGH FEELINGS OF LOSS

Tasks, stories and exercises designed specifically to help a child to find, think about, and work through a range of healthy options in coping with feelings of loss

This section is designed to provide a whole host of ideas to enable children to speak about their loss in unthreatening, child-friendly ways. Children need help with a language for grief, as do many adults! So these exercises enable children to speak about their grief and loss in richer, more specific ways, rather than just saying that they are sad. The exercises may also help the children to speak about the intensity of their feelings. We also highly recommend reading to the child the story that accompanies this book. It is called *The Day the Sea Went Out and Never Came Back*.

Children often cannot speak clearly and fully in everyday language about what they are feeling, but by and large they can show or enact, or draw or play out their feelings very well indeed. However, they need to be given the right language of expression. For some it is writing, for others it might be drawing, puppet-play, or using miniature toys in a sandbox. Therefore, many of the exercises in this section offer support for creative and imaginative ways of expression. There are also some tasks to ensure that you do not get into asking the child lots of questions, which he could find threatening. So some of the tasks just require a tick in a box, or a quick colouring-in, or choice of a word or image from a selection.

Please note: The tasks and exercises are not designed to be worked through in chronological order. Also, there are far too many to attempt them all in one go: the child could feel bombarded. So just pick those you think would be right for the particular child you are working with, taking into account their age, and how defended or undefended they are about talking about their feelings of loss.

Direct instructions to the child are in the tinted boxes.

✳ The 'Losing too Much' story

Finish this story with drawings. It is about a creature who loses someone very precious to him.

Draw what happens to him in the next few boxes. If you need more boxes for your story, just add them.

Figure 13 The 'Losing Too Much' story

✳ The place of too much empty

What does the world feel like when you've lost someone or something lovely and very precious? Tick or colour in the picture below if it feels like any of these. You can tick more than one.

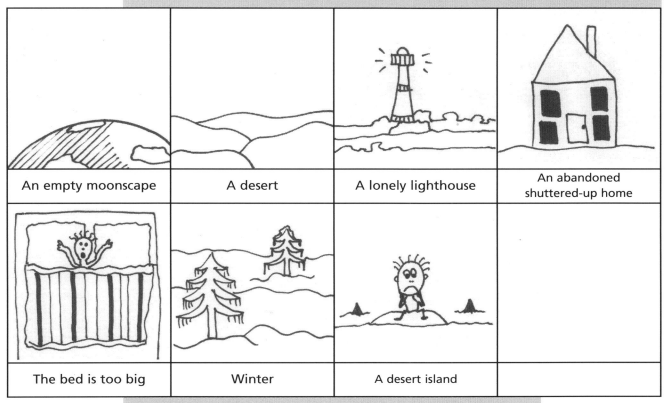

An empty moonscape	A desert	A lonely lighthouse	An abandoned shuttered-up home
The bed is too big	Winter	A desert island	

If it wasn't any of these, draw or write your own.

Figure 14
The place of too
much empty

✳ Sad stories

It is often helpful to children to read stories in which a child or creature suffers a terrible loss. It can make their own feelings seem far more understandable. There are also many useful stories of lost souls, and stories of lost souls found and saved.

Do any of these stories feel a bit like the sad story of what has happened to you? Tick if any of them do.

- ⚙ The pet that gets left behind when the family move house. ☐

- ⚙ The killing of Bambi's mother, leaving Bambi without a mummy. ☐

- ⚙ The children left behind when Mary Poppins flies away with her umbrella. ☐

- ⚙ Little Portly the otter getting lost in *Wind in the Willows*. ☐

- ⚙ The death of Aslan the lion in CS Lewis's *Narnia* tales. ☐

- ⚙ Cinderella. ☐

- ⚙ Hansel and Gretel. ☐

- ⚙ The Little Match Girl looking in the window, left out in the cold. ☐

If it is none of these, is there another story you know which is like a sad story in your life?

✳ Before and after pictures

This exercise involves sandplay. You will need a sandbox with a large selection of miniatures and objects. See the book *Using Storytelling as a Therapeutic Tool for Children* (Sunderland, 2001), if you need more information on how to use sandplay.

Using the miniature objects and figures, show in the sandbox what life was like before you lost this person.

Show in the sandbox or in a painting what it feels like now you have lost this person.

✳ **Shock pictures**

When the person you loved left or died, it can feel like a terrible shock. If this happened to you, did the shock feel like any of these? Tick or colour in one or more of the boxes if it did.

If it felt like something else, draw or write what it felt like in the empty box.

A door slammed in your face	Everything falling out of everything	A punch in your gut	A great smash
A terrible noise	Everything coming to a standstill	The world coming to an end	

Figure 15 Shock pictures

Helping Children with Loss © M Sunderland & N Armstrong 2003

✳ Life after losing

Now that your life has changed because of your loss, does it ever feel like any of these things? Colour in or tick the ones it feels like.

Like you have been shipwrecked on a desert island	Being buried alive	Being in a hole with no hands to reach in and help you out
Being in a world with no warm faces in it	Being in a world where it is always winter	

Figure 16 Life after losing

If it is none of these, draw how it has changed in the empty box.

✳ Pain drain

The feelings below are feelings people can have when someone they loved very very much then leaves or dies. If you have any of these feelings, colour them in or tick the box.

Too full of silent screams	Too full of uncried tears	Wanting to give up	Like you just want to sleep forever
Feeling nothing, but it is a horrid kind of nothing	Very angry	Like you want to hurt or punish them for leaving you or dying	Guilt that somehow it was your fault that they are gone
Like your heart is broken	Just longing to be cuddled up again in the person who has left you	Frightened by your pain	

If it is none of these, draw in the empty box what it feels like after your loss.

Figure 17
Pain drain

Helping Children with Loss © M Sunderland & N Armstrong 2003

Speechmark

✳ Leaving or dying – when you knew it was going to happen

> As the ship drew further away and [Alcyone's] eyes could not distinguish his features, her gaze still followed the departing vessel as long as possible. Then, when even the ship was too far away to be clearly seen, she still watched the sails billowing out from the masthead. Finally not even the sails were visible, and she sought her empty couch where she lay down with a heavy heart. Her bed and her surroundings made her weep afresh, reminding her what part of herself she had lost. (Ovid, 1995, p66)

This exercise is for children who have lost someone whom they knew would leave them or die, as opposed to the rupture of a sudden death or unannounced leaving.

⊚ Draw or scribble the feelings you had from the first time you knew the person you loved was going to leave you.

⊚ Draw or scribble the feelings you had in your last time together.

⊚ Draw your feelings now that they have gone.

✳ 'The Place of Not-Enough' and 'The Place of More-Than-Enough'

- ◉ Make a sandpicture of 'The Place of Not-Enough' or draw a picture of it.

- ◉ Then make a sandpicture of 'The Place of More-Than-Enough' or draw a picture of it.

- ◉ What do you feel, being in 'The Place of Not-Enough'?

- ◉ Pick a miniature figure to be you, and put yourself in 'The Place of Not Enough'. Show what you do there and feel there.

- ◉ Then move the you-figure to 'The Place of More-Than-Enough'. Show what you do there and feel there. Who is there? Who is not there?

- ◉ Now, using the you-figure, tell a story of how you get from 'The Place of Not-Enough' to 'The Place of More-Than-Enough'.

Speechmark Ⓢ Ⓟ This page may be photocopied for instructional use only.

Helping Children with Loss © M Sunderland & N Armstrong 2003

69

✳ The very missed person in your mind

Draw the person you miss very much. Draw how you see them in your mind.

If they were a colour, what would the colour be? Draw it.

If they were a thing, what would they be? Draw it.

If they were an animal, what would they be? Draw it.

And if you were an animal with them, what would you be? Draw it.

And now they are gone, what animal do you feel like now? Draw it.

If they were a food, what would the food be? Draw it.

If they were a place, what would the place be? Draw it.

Now think of the person you loved, and see if you can describe what you especially like about that person in a drawing. Draw it.

In this exercise, one child drew his depressed, emotionally unavailable father as a patch of fog. Another drew her dead Mummy as a tiny Mummy figure, just a speck on the horizon: 'She has gone too far out.' Another bereaved child drew the Mummy in his mind as a lovely soft pillow.

✳ Missing too much

Draw what it feels like inside you when you are missing the person too much.

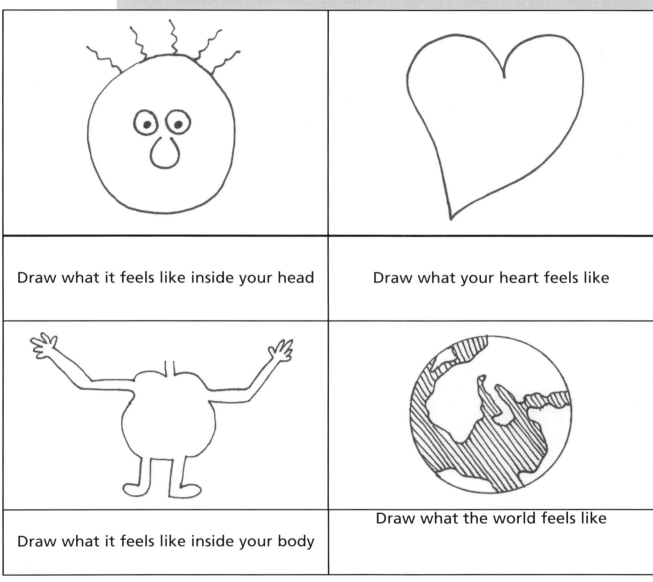

Draw what it feels like inside your head	Draw what your heart feels like
Draw what it feels like inside your body	Draw what the world feels like

Figure 18
Missing too much

71

✳ 'Museum of Lovely Times'

Again, this exercise is for children whose loved person has left or died.

Enter the 'Museum of Lovely Times'. Draw or write on the museum exhibit stands some of the lovely times you shared together. Tell the grown-up with you about these times if you want to.

You might have hoarded these memories deep in your mind, but if you talk about, or show or draw, them, it can help you to feel warmer inside. These lovely memories are like treasures, and no-one can ever take them away from you. But if you hoard them too deep down in your mind and very rarely, if ever, bring them out, they may get all cobwebby and, like that, they cannot warm you.

It is as if you know two worlds at the moment. One is the lovely world you had together, and the lovely moments you shared. The other is the world without that lovely person. It is good to feel your feelings about both worlds. But do it with someone there to listen, so it can feel safe and far less scary and lonely.

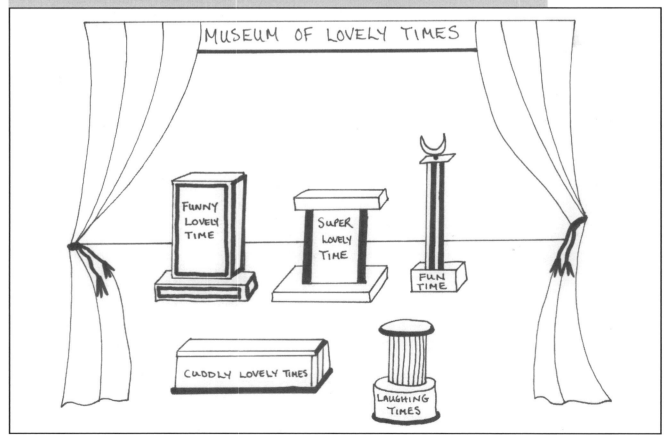

Figure 19 'Museum of Lovely Times'

✳ Your life as a house

Draw all the most important things or people in your life in the six rooms of loveliness – the things in your life that make it warm and good, and worth living.

Then, in the Attic of Special Memories, draw or write the loveliest memories you have. Who were you with? If you like, draw them there too.

In the Basement of Banishment, draw or write the people or things in your life that are making your life hard or miserable. If you really hate someone or something, and wish they would go away forever, put them in the dustbin or on the fire. Draw or write them there.

In the New Hope Building, draw the people, things, dreams or plans that you would like to be part of your life. They may be part of your life in some way already, but you would like them to have a bigger place in your life.

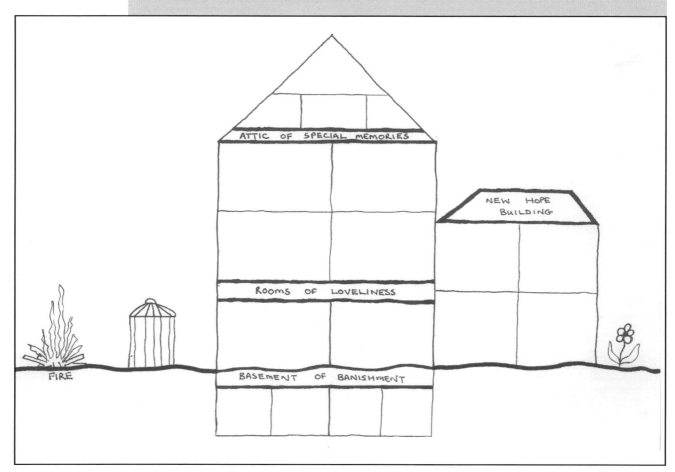

Figure 20 Your life as a house

WHY THERAPY OR COUNSELLING FOR CHILDREN WHO HAVE LOST SOMEONE THEY LOVE?

How therapy and counselling can enable a child to grieve

> Give sorrow words: the grief that does not speak, whispers the o'er fraught heart and bids it break. (Shakespeare, *Macbeth*, 4.3.209–10)

Shakespeare knew only too well that if grief is left unspoken, all bottled up inside, it can cause long-lasting psychological pain, resulting in all manner of emotional or behavioural problems. Indeed, research shows that much mental illness is caused by the repression or suppression of grief. For example, as we have seen, the biggest group of children under nine to be excluded from school have all been bereaved (Home Office, 2001). Research also shows that bereaved children, if not helped, can fall behind in school (van Eerdewegh *et al*, 1985).

However, with the right help, the child who suffers a tragic loss does not need to face mental ill-health. As Wolpert, psychiatrist and author of the excellent book *Malignant Sadness* states, 'There is no compelling reason to believe that the death of a parent itself, no matter how distressing at the time, is a risk factor [for vulnerability to depression in later life]. What really matters is how the death is handled and the parenting and care in the ensuing period' (Wolpert, 1999, p53).

If the child is able to speak and grieve about his loss with someone who can stay with his pain without trying to persuade him out of it, then he can move forward in life from a position of emotional health. But if this does not happen, it is indeed a risk factor for vulnerability to depression in later life, or other neurotic symptoms, or being stuck in anger, or indeed mind-blindness in the parenting of his *own* child's distress states.

Therapy or counselling can enable a child who has suffered a painful loss to:

✳ Feel safe to grieve and to work through deep feelings of fear and mistrust about loving, so that he can dare to love again. As Bowlby says, 'We can only really mourn in the presence of another.' (1973, p172)

✳ Have real time to talk about their lost loved person as an emotionally healthy way of staying connected with them.

✳ Help a child to dare to feel the pain of loss in order to be able to grieve. As Shakespeare said of Ophelia who went mad from grief, 'As one incapable of her own distress.' Many children who have lost someone they love deeply are incapable of their own distress too. They need help. Without help, it is so understandable that a child cuts himself off from his grief, resulting in all manner of physical or neurotic symptoms, aggressive behaviour, self-destructive behaviour, or an emotional numbing that stifles too much of the child's life-force. Without a therapist, the pain is often far too much and far too deep to go it alone. The mind's defence mechanisms will often make sure of that!

✳ When the loss of the loved one has left a deep mistrust about love and the pain it can bring, then the empathy and compassion provided by the therapeutic relationship can free the child to be able to dare to love again. Therapy can enable a child to work through his linking of love with psychological danger – for example, the fear of more rejection, more abandonment, more shock, more catastrophic disappointment.

How therapy and counselling can ensure that the tragic loss does not leave the child with post-traumatic stress

> The bereaved yearn and are preoccupied with their loss; the traumatized are anxious and preoccupied with their trauma ... The bereaved seek out associations with their loved one; the traumatised avoid reminders of the event ... The bereaved dream of their dead ... The traumatised suffer nightmares, experiencing terror rather than loss. (Harris-Hendriks *et al*, 2000, p44)

In order that the loss does not become a trauma, children may need therapy to deal with feelings of shock and helplessness before they are able to mourn fully. In other words, some children may need therapy to help them to get to the stage where they *can* grieve.

What happens in therapy when a child works through the grief?

Therapy, when a child works through his grief, it is about 'summoning up reminders of the dead parent and grieving for them one by one' (Harris-Hendriks *et al*, 2000, p44). It is about being able to linger over memories of the lost one. It's about having a place and real quality time to speak at length (through words and images) of the terrible pain of the yearning, missing, disappointment of no more shared times together, the anger and protest about what has happened.

As we have seen, because children often do not have the words to express their grief; because they get so absorbed in the moment of what they are doing or playing, and because they have such strong motoric impulses to move about, to express things through movement, it is easy to be deceived about their grieving and even to think, 'Oh well, maybe because they are children they do not need to grieve.'

Why therapy and counselling are especially important for a child who is left with no loving comforting adult after their loss

Children who are left with no loving, comforting adult after their loss should be prioritised in terms of being given school counselling or therapy. The pain of losing a loved one is all the more agonising if the child has no other loved parent figure to whom he can turn for comfort. Then his world is truly one of wilderness.

BIBLIOGRAPHY

Alvarez A, 1971, *The Savage God: A Study of Suicide*, Penguin, Harmondsworth.

American Psychiatric Association, 1994, *Diagnostic and Statistical Manual of Mental Disorders: DSM-IV* 4th edn, American Psychiatric Association, Washington.

Bowlby J, 1973, *Attachment and Loss: Volume 2 – Separation, Anxiety and Anger*, Hogarth Press, London.

Bowlby J, 1978, *Attachment and Loss: Volume 3 – Loss, Sadness and Depression*, Penguin, Harmondsworth.

Bowlby J, 1979, *The Making and Breaking of Affectional Bonds*, Tavistock, London.

Bowlby J, 1988, *A Secure Base: Clinical Applications of Attachment Theory*, Routledge, London.

Buber M, 1987, *I and Thou* (Gregor Smith R trans), T & T Clark, Edinburgh. (First published 1937.)

Byatt AS, 1995, *Still Life*, Vintage, New York/London.

Clarkson P, 1989, *Gestalt Counselling in Action*, Sage, London.

Coleman J, 1999, *Key Data on Adolescence,* Trust for the Study of Adolescence, London.

Dinnage R, 1990, *The Ruffian on the Stair: Reflections on Death*, Viking, London.

Eerdewegh MM van, Clayton PJ & Eerdewegh P van, 1985, 'The Bereaved Child: Variables Influencing Early Psychopathology', *British Journal of Psychiatry* 147, pp188–94.

Eliot TS, 1990, *Collected Poems 1909–1962*, Faber & Faber, London. (Original work published 1936 as *Collected Poems*.)

Evans C & Millard A, 1995, *Greek Myths and Legends*, Usborne, London.

Freud S, 1979, 'Inhibitions, Symptoms and Anxiety', in *On Psychopathology, Inhibitions, Symptoms and Anxiety*, Vol 10 of *The Penguin Freud Library*, Richards A & Strachey J (eds), Strachey J (trans), Penguin, Harmondsworth, pp237–333. (First published 1926.)

Freud S, 1984, 'Mourning and Melancholia', *On Metapsychology: The Theory of Psychoanalysis,* Vol 11 of *The Pelican Freud Library,* Penguin, London, pp245–68. (First published 1917.)

Freud S, 1991, 'General Theory of the Neuroses', *Introductory Lectures on Psychoanalysis*, Vol 1 of *The Penguin Freud Library*, Richards A & Strachey J (eds), Strachey J (trans), Penguin, Harmondsworth, pp281–517. (First published 1917.)

Fristad MA, Jedel R, Weller RA & Weller EB, 1993, 'Psychosocial Functioning in Children after the Death of a Parent', *American Journal of Psychiatry* 150(3), pp511–13.

Goodall J, 1990, *Through a Window: Thirty Years with the Chimpanzees of Gombe*, Weidenfeld & Nicolson, London.

Harlow HF & Mears C, 1979, *Primate Perspectives*, John Wiley, New York/London.

Harris-Hendriks J, 1993, *When Father Kills Mother: Guiding Children Through Trauma and Grief*, Routledge, London.

Heinicke C & Westheimer I, 1966, *Brief Separations*, International Universities Press, New York.

Herman N, 1987, *Why Psychotherapy?*, Free Association Books, London.

Hopkins GM, 1985, *Poems and Prose*, Gardner WH (ed), Penguin, Harmondsworth. (First published 1918.)

Klein M, 1988a, *Envy and Gratitude and Other Works 1946–1963*, Virago, London.

Klein M, 1988b, 'Love, Guilt and Reparation', *Love, Guilt and Reparation and Other Works 1921–1945*, Virago, London, pp306–43.

Klein M, 1988c, 'The Psychotherapy of the Psychoses', *Love, Guilt and Reparation and Other Works 1921–1945*, Virago, London, pp233–5.

Kotulak R, 1997, *Inside The Brain: Revolutionary Discoveries of How the Mind Works*, Andrews McMeel Publishing, Kansas City.

Lewis CS, 1966, *A Grief Observed*, Faber & Faber, London. (First published 1961.)

Levi P, 1986, *Moments of Reprieve*, Feldman R (trans), Abacus, London.

Levi P, 1987, *If This is a Man/The Truce*, Abacus, London. (First published 1958.)

Masters B, 1985, *Killing for Company: The Case of Dennis Nilsen*, Cape, London.

Mental Health Foundation, 1999, *The Fundamental Facts: All the Latest Facts and Figures on Mental Illness*, Mental Health Foundation, London.

Mitchell S, 1988, *Relational Concepts in Psychoanalysis: An Integration*, Guildford, New York.

Montagu A, 1971, *Touching: The Human Significance of the Skin*, Harper & Row, London.

Moore T, 1992, *Care of the Soul: A Guide for Cultivating Depth and Sacredness in Everyday Life*, HarperCollins, New York.

Murray L, 1997, *Subhuman Redneck Poems*, Carcanet, Manchester.

Orbach S, 1994, *What's Really Going On Here?* Virago, London.

Ovid, 1995, *Orpheus in the Underworld*, Innes M (trans), Penguin, Harmondsworth.

Panksepp J, 1998, *Affective Neuroscience: The Foundations of Human and Animal Emotions*, Oxford University Press, Oxford.

Plath S, 1981, *Collected Poems*, Faber & Faber, London.

Plato, 1951, *The Symposium*, Hamilton W (trans), Penguin, Harmondsworth.

Reid S, 1990, 'The Importance of Beauty in the Psychoanalytic Experience', *Journal of Child Psychotherapy* 16(1), pp29–52. (Originally given at a study weekend of the Association of Child Psychotherapists, March 1987.)

Rilke RM, 1939, *The Duino Elegies*, Leishman JB & Spender S (trans), WW Norton, New York.

Robertson J, 1953, 'A Two-Year-Old Goes to Hospital', Penn State Audio-Visual Services, University Park PA.

Stern DN, 1993, 'Acting Versus Remembering in Transference Love and Infantile Love', Spector Person E, Hagelin A and Fonagy P (eds), *On Freud's 'Observations on Transference-Love'*, New Haven/London: Yale University Press, pp172–85.

Strachey A (ed), 1907, *The Letters of Edward Lear*, Fisher Unwin, London.

Sunderland M & Armstrong N, 2003, *The Day the Sea Went Out and Never Came Back*, Speechmark Publishing, Brackley.

Sunderland M, 2001, *Using Storytelling as a Therapeutic Tool with Children*, Speechmark Publishing, Brackley.

Winnicott DW, 1996, 'The Effect of Loss on The Young', Shepherd R, Johns J & Robinson HT (eds), *D. W. Winnicott: Thinking About Children*, Karnac, London, pp46–7. (First published 1968.)

Wolpert L, 1999, *Malignant Sadness: The Anatomy of Depression*, Faber & Faber, London.

Woodman M, 1985, *The Pregnant Virgin: A Process of Psychological Transformation*, Inner City Books, Toronto, CA.

Helping Children with Feelings
Margot Sunderland, illustrated by Nicky Armstrong

This is a ground-breaking pack of nine beautifully illustrated stories which have been designed to help children who are troubled in their lives. The stories act as vehicles to help children think about and connect with their feelings. Each is accompanied by a guidebook that will prove a vital resource when using the stories. Featured below are details about five of the titles and an accompanying handbook.

Using Story Telling as a Therapeutic Tool with Children

This practical manual begins with the philosophy and psychology underpinning the therapeutic value of story telling. It shows how to use story telling as a therapeutic tool with children and how to make an effective response when a child tells a story to you. It is an essential accompaniment to the series: Helping Children with Feelings. Covers such issues as:

◆ Why story telling is such a good way of helping children with their feelings;

◆ What resources you may need in a story-telling session;

◆ How to construct your own therapeutic story for a child;

◆ What to do when children tell stories to you;

◆ Things to do and things to say when working with a child's story.

108pp, illustrated, paperback
Order code: 002-4720

Willy and the Wobbly House
Helping children who are anxious or obsessional

Willy is an anxious boy who experiences the world as a very unsafe wobbly place where anything awful might happen at any time. Joe, the boy next door, is too ordered and tidy to be able to ever really enjoy life. Willy longs for order while Joe longs for things to wobble. However, when they meet Mrs Flop she tells them they don't have to put up with feeling as they do. At her suggestion they visit the Puddle People who help them break out of their fixed patterns and find far richer ways of living in the world.

Storybook: 32pp, A4, full colour throughout, wire-stitched
Guidebook: 60pp, A4, illustrated, wire-o-bound
Order code: 002-4774

The Frog Who Longed for the Moon to Smile
Helping children who yearn for someone they love

Frog is very much in love with the moon because the moon once smiled at him. Now he spends all his time gazing at the moon and dreaming about her. He waits and waits for her to smile at him again. One day a wise and friendly crow helps Frog to see how he is wasting his life away. Eventually Frog takes the huge step of turning away from the moon. When he does, he feels a terrible emptiness and loneliness. He has not yet seen what is on the other side of him. When in time he looks around, he is lit up by everything he sees. All the time he has been facing the place of very little, he's had his back to the place of plenty.

Storybook: 32pp, A4, full colour throughout, wire-stitched
Guidebook: 48pp, A4, illustrated, wire-o-bound
Order code: 002-4776

A Nifflenoo Called Nevermind
Helping children who bottle up their feelings

Nevermind always carries on whatever happens! Each time something horrible happens to him he is very brave and simply says 'never mind'. He meets with all kinds of setbacks, bullying and disappointments but each time he just tucks his feelings away and carries on with life. However, he becomes so full of bottled-up feelings that after a time he gets stuck in a hedge. In addition, some of these feelings start to leak out of him in ways that hurt others. Luckily he happens upon a bogwert who helps him understand that his feelings do matter and should not be ignored. Nifflenoo then learns how to both express his feelings and stand up for himself.

Storybook: 36pp, A4, full colour throughout, wire-stitched
Guidebook: 48pp, A4, illustrated, wire-o-bound
Order code: 002-4775

A Pea Called Mildred
Helping children pursue their hopes and dreams

Mildred is a pea with dreams. She has great plans for her pea life. However, people are always telling her that her dreams are pointless as she is just another ordinary pea. As she is not prepared to be just another ordinary pea and let go of her dreams, she goes into a very lonely place. Eventually, with the help of a kind person along the way, Mildred ends up doing exactly what she has always dreamed of doing.

Storybook: 28pp, A4, full colour throughout, wire-stitched
Guidebook: 28pp, A4, illustrated, wire-o-bound
Order code: 002-4777

A Wibble Called Bipley (and a Few Honks)
Helping children who have hardened their hearts or become bullies

Bipley is a warm cuddly creature, but the trouble is someone has broken his heart. He feels so hurt that he decides it is just too painful to ever love again. When he meets some big tough Honks in the wood, they teach him how to harden his heart so that he doesn't have to feel hurt anymore. Bipley turns into a bully. To begin with he feels powerful but gradually he realises that the world has turned terribly grey. Luckily, Bipley meets some creatures who teach him how he can protect himself without hardening his heart.

Storybook: 44pp, A4, full colour throughout, wire-stitched
Guidebook: 60pp, A4, illustrated, wire-o-bound
Order code: 002-4778

**70 Alston Drive • Bradwell Abbey
Milton Keynes MK13 9HG • UK
Tel: +44 (0) 1908 326944
Fax: +44 (0) 1908 326960
www.speechmark.net**